D1083978

# THE FLAG AND THE CROSS

# THE FLAG AND THE CROSS

White Christian Nationalism and the Threat to
American Democracy

Philip S. Gorski

AND

Samuel L. Perry

Foreword by Jemar Tisby

OXFORD
UNIVERSITY PRESS

## OXFORD
### UNIVERSITY PRESS

Oxford University Press is a department of the University of Oxford. It furthers
the University's objective of excellence in research, scholarship, and education
by publishing worldwide. Oxford is a registered trade mark of Oxford University
Press in the UK and certain other countries.

Published in the United States of America by Oxford University Press
198 Madison Avenue, New York, NY 10016, United States of America.

Library of Congress Control Number: 2021923315
ISBN 978-0-19-761868-4

DOI: 10.1093/oso/9780197618684.001.0001

3 5 7 9 8 6 4

Printed by LSC Communications, United States of America

# CONTENTS

# FOREWORD

I thought I had endured the worst racism that Christians could spew at me. Then came November 2016.

In a bracing turn of events, a minority of voters elected Donald J. Trump as the 45th president of the United States. To add to the head-spinning element of the moment, exit polls showed that white evangelical Christians who voted had pulled the lever for Trump at a rate of about 81 percent.

I remember staying up late on election night as the results rolled in. I sat alone, my wife having long since gone to bed with the resolution that seeing the results live on television would not change the outcome. It was dark and I was toggling my eyes between the television screen and the Twitter feed on my phone. When it was clear that Trump had won, it became nearly impossible for me to grab and hold onto a single thought as my mind and emotions struggled to keep up with this new development.

Finally, a feeling of dread settled over me as I reckoned with the fact that a blatant opponent of racial justice would soon occupy the highest political office in our nation. Then my thoughts focused on matters closer to home: my church. I attended a congregation that was predominantly white and evangelical. By the percentages and from my own interactions with them, I knew that many of my fellow churchgoers had voted for Trump. I couldn't shake the pain I felt. I had made no secret about my concerns about this man, particularly his long record of trafficking in racial stereotypes and coddling racists.

How could I go to church that Sunday with people who so clearly misunderstood and perhaps even dismissed my reality as a Black person in America? How could I sing, pray, and exchange pleasantries with folks who seemed not to care what their favored politician's plans would mean for me, my family, our community, and our country? I knew I wouldn't be able to fake it, and I didn't want to try.

None of what I was feeling was unique to me. From my work with Black Christians all over the country, I knew that many others had similar misgivings about their faith communities leading up to and in the wake of the presidential election. While they may have shared their concerns privately with trusted friends and family members, I went and turned on the mic to record a podcast.

My friend Beau interviewed me about my reactions to the election and I spoke honestly. I said, "I don't feel safe worshiping at my predominantly white evangelical church this Sunday." I went on to describe the sense of betrayal I felt from white evangelicals as a whole, but how I still valued individual white Christians for their commitments to racial justice. I sensed my words would sound jarring to some, so I spoke with as much nuance as I could muster.

It didn't help.

Not long after we released the podcast episode, my mentions on social media turned into a dumpster fire of racist jabs and diatribes.

One meme depicted a cartoonish young Black man shaking hands with a chimpanzee while the caption called me a "woke n***a." Another called me a "wokevangelical." On a follow-up blog post I wrote, someone else commented that I was merely engaging in "moral posturing" and had succumbed to the "ethically paralyzing and emotionalized position of racial solidarity and sympathy." A fellow church member—one with whom I had never had an in-depth conversation—commented on Twitter that my views on Christianity, Trump, and the election were "liberal" and "worldly." In the aftermath, several think pieces appeared that criticized me, and the denomination and religious communities of which I was a part quickly became sites of marginalization and ostracism.

For three weeks, I could not go online without the little muscle under my left eye twitching. The stress had caused a physiological response in which I essentially winced every time I opened my laptop. I became conditioned to expect the worst; and when I thought the rhetoric couldn't spiral any lower, it always did. I later learned that what I experienced is a form of racial trauma, and several years later I am still processing its effects through therapy, prayer, and reflection.

I think part of why the criticism affected me so deeply was that I couldn't name exactly the forces that were acting against me. I didn't have a category to explain the toxic combination of racism, religion, and politics that had taken over my life.

That's where learning about white Christian nationalism and the work of Philip Gorski, Samuel Perry, and other scholars researching the subject helped so much. The concept of white Christian nationalism encompasses the many ways bigotry, prejudice, xenophobia, patriarchy, and racism show up in Christian guise. More than merely providing a nomenclature for a sociocultural phenomenon, white Christian nationalism helps explain the mindsets and beliefs that lead to certain behaviors that seem so contradictory.

How could self-described born-again Christians who placed so much emphasis on morality champion a philandering, arrogant, and cruel politician like Donald Trump? How did wearing a mask during a viral pandemic become an issue of "religious freedom?" Why did so many Christians who quote Romans 13 about being subject to the governing authorities support an attempted insurrection at the Capitol building? Do racism and white supremacy form the subtext of all their beliefs?

The answers to these questions are historical, contextual, and complex. But *The Flag and the Cross* offers a glimpse into a system that has an internal, if frustrating, logic of its own. Gorski and Perry give clear and deeply researched examinations of critical ideas such as Christian libertarianism as well as idiosyncratic notions of order, freedom, and the use of violence. The authors go further. They show how white Christian nationalism is not simply a set of beliefs, but a narrative—a "deep story" that keeps getting told, re-told, and embellished to suit the desires of those who buy into it.

*The Flag and the Cross* leaves us with a dire but necessary warning. While it would be comforting to think of the insurrection at the Capitol as an isolated event that won't be repeated in the near future, the data that Gorski and Perry compiled lead in a different direction. They conclude that not only is another violent power grab possible, but "A second eruption would likely be larger and more violent than the first. Large enough to bury American democracy for at least a generation." And maybe longer.

Others concur with their assessment. In 2020 the Department of Homeland Security issued its annual Homeland Threat Assessment. Officials warned that "Among Domestic Violent Extremists (DVEs), racially and ethnically motivated violent extremists— specifically white supremacist extremists (WSEs)—will remain the most persistent and lethal threat in the Homeland." Although white supremacist extremists and white Christian nationalists are not identical, there is some overlap and, like the Ku Klux Klan and similar groups, white supremacist extremists easily co-opt Christian symbols and ideas for violent purposes. Given the historic and ongoing dangers posed by white Christian nationalism and its related movements, Gorski and Perry insist on urgently and aggressively combating this ideology.

The convincing research presented in *The Flag and the Cross* has led me to the following assessment: white Christian nationalism is the greatest threat to the witness of the church in the United States today. It is not, as many white Christian nationalists would contend, Critical Race Theory or the 1619 Project or wokeness that push people away from the church and hinders democracy—white Christian nationalism does that.

The information in *The Flag and the Cross* may not convince the white Christian nationalists in your midst to change their minds or their actions. This book will, however, give you more confidence to engage different, and often pernicious, viewpoints from an informed perspective. You can use the quotes from Paul Weyrich found in the book to describe how making it harder to vote has been an intentional strategy of white Christian nationalists to maintain political power. You can point out the plethora of Christian symbols at the Capitol insurrection and ask why so many thought that Christ himself sanctioned their actions. You can cite statistical data and polling numbers to show how xenophobia, a narrow interpretation of "we the people," and an aversion to structural explanations of inequality are all positively correlated to white Christian nationalism.

Although our specific stories may differ, we have all been affected by white Christian nationalism. There may be people in your church or faith community who adhere to its principles. Perhaps you have family members, co-workers, or friends you've had to confront or even cut off because of this malicious ideology. You may have had to leave a space where you thought you belonged because you refused to parrot the party line. Everyone in the United States has to deal with the threats that white Christian nationalism poses to civil rights and democracy itself.

Since the impact of white Christian nationalism is so ubiquitous, *The Flag and the Cross* is not a book you can simply read—the knowledge this book imparts must be absorbed and applied. We all have to be able to spot white Christian nationalism in everyday life, current events, legislative actions, and rhetoric. We have to become adept at addressing white Christian nationalism when and where we see it. This will take a rare kind of courage that stands against the status quo at great risk to oneself. But we have no other choice: the stakes are too high. Apathy and indifference make us complicit in the demise of our nation. We must use the data assembled by Gorski and Perry in *The Flag and the Cross* to fight white Christian nationalism as if our entire democracy depends on it. Indeed, it does.

Jemar Tisby

# Introduction

## *Eruption*

The chaos of the Capitol insurrection on January 6, 2021, was bewildering for many. In part, because the violent riot was also a riot of images: a wooden cross and a wooden gallows; Christian flags and Confederate flags; "Jesus Saves" and "Don't Tread on Me" banners; button-down shirts and bullet-proof vests.[1] But these confusing—and even seemingly contradictory—symbols are part of an increasingly familiar ideology: "white Christian nationalism."[2]

This book is a primer on white Christian nationalism, what it is, when it emerged, how it works, and where it's headed. White Christian nationalism is one of the oldest and most powerful currents in American politics. But until the insurrection, it was invisible to most Americans. It was invisible to most conservative white Christians, because for decades it has been the water they swim in and the air they breathe.[3] It was invisible to most secular progressives, because they live in a bubble of their own in which white Christian nationalism seems "fringe" rather than mainstream.

*1*

But that bubble was burst on January 6, 2021, by the white-hot rage of pro-Trump insurrectionists. That rage had been building since long before the presidential election. Throughout 2020, President Trump routinely spouted debunked claims of mail-in ballots from pets, dead people, and undocumented immigrants, virtually promising rampant voter fraud come November.[4] Following his election loss, he desperately stoked his followers' rage via Twitter, sowing lies about a stolen election. His efforts were fanned by pro-Trump pundits on the Christian right and loyal congressional allies like Ted Cruz, Josh Hawley, and Matt Gaetz who helped propagate his "Big Lie."

The Capitol insurrection was like the eruption of a volcano. The pressure had been building for decades. The election simply sent that pressure shooting toward the surface, where it erupted into violence on January 6. The buildup was partly the result of propaganda and fear-mongering facilitated by increased polarization, foreign interference in elections, and the social media revolution. But it was also the result of slow-moving demographic and cultural transitions. The numerical influence of conservative white Protestants is declining.[5] The US population is becoming less white and more secular. The nation has become less powerful and more unequal. The tectonic plates of history were colliding with each other, creating new fissures and mounting tensions. The election of Barack Obama was one result of these gradual shifts; the unexpected victory of Donald Trump another; the Capitol insurrection yet a third. There are more to come.[6]

Geologists study volcanic eruptions for four reasons: (1) to understand the shape of the landscape, (2) to uncover the forces that have formed it, (3) to explain why they erupt when they do, and (4) to forecast eruptions and avoid catastrophes.

We are sociologists, but we follow the geologists' lead. We begin by mapping the landscape of contemporary white Christian nationalism: what it is and is not, who does and does not adhere to it, and what they do and do not believe. We then drill down below the surface, through the various layers of white Christian nationalism that have built up over time to the biblical bedrock on which it rests. After that, we take a closer look at the role white Christian nationalism has played in American politics in recent years, both as an ideology and as a political strategy, from the Obama presidency and the rise of the Tea Party; through Trump's election, presidency, and failed re-election; to the attempted insurrection of 2021. We conclude with predictions about America's future, and how we can avoid "the big one," a political earthquake that could topple American democracy.

## OUR ARGUMENTS

In this book, we address four fundamental questions: (1) What is white Christian nationalism? (2) When did it emerge? (3) How does it work politically? And, finally (4) Where might it be headed tomorrow?

White Christian nationalism is a "deep story" about America's past and a vision of its future. It includes cherished assumptions about what America was and is, but also what it *should* be. We borrow the "deep story" idea from sociologist Arlie Russell Hochschild. In her 2016 book *Strangers in Their Own Land*, she recounts the lessons she learned during the five years she spent talking with white working-class Americans in the oil-refining regions of rural Louisiana.[7] Their "deep story" goes something like this: people like them have been standing in line, waiting patiently for their chance at the American dream. But up ahead, they see people cutting in line—immigrants and minorities and other people who haven't paid their dues. What's worse, they see politicians helping the line-cutters, liberal politicians like Barack Obama and Hillary Clinton. So, they vote for conservative politicians who (they believe) will send those people to the back of the line where they belong. The unstated (and incorrect) assumption is that "white people were here first." The deep story sounds a lot like "Make American Great Again." It helps explain why so many rural whites voted for Donald Trump in 2016, and again in 2020.[8]

What makes deep stories "stories" is that they function like a bare-bones movie script. They include a cast of heroes and villains, and well-worn and familiar plots that events are supposed to follow. And, like many classic scripts, they are made and remade, with tweaked storylines and new leading men.

What makes deep stories "deep" is that they have deep roots in a culture. Deep stories have been told and retold so many times and across so many generations that they feel natural and true: even and perhaps especially when they are at odds with history. In sum, a deep story is more myth than history. More precisely, it is a mythological version of history.

White Christian nationalism's "deep story" goes something like this: America was founded as a Christian nation by (white) men who were "traditional" Christians, who based the nation's founding documents on "Christian principles." The United States is blessed by God, which is why it has been so successful; and the nation has a special role to play in God's plan for humanity. But these blessings are threatened by cultural degradation from "un-American" influences both inside and outside our borders.

Like any story, this one has its heroes: white conservative Christians, usually native-born men. It also has its villains: racial, religious, and cultural outsiders. The plot revolves around conflicts between the noble and worthy "us," the rightful heirs of wealth and power, and the undeserving "them" who conspire to take what is ours. Sometimes, the conflicts culminate in violence—violence that restores white Christians to what they believe is their rightful place atop America's racial and religious hierarchy. The heroes are those who defend the purity—and property—of the white Christian nation: with violence, when necessary.

But this story is a myth. The religious views of the Founders ranged widely: from atheism through deism and Unitarianism to Congregationalism, Baptism, and even Roman Catholicism. The Declaration and the Constitution drew on various influences, including classical liberalism (e.g., Locke) and civic republicanism (e.g., Machiavelli). More than a little of the nation's wealth and prosperity were derived from stolen land and slave labor. These are all well-established historical facts.[9]

At this point, the skeptical reader might wonder what's "Christian" about this deep story. It is "Christian" because the vast majority of those who believe this story identify as such. It is also "Christian" insofar as it draws on particular readings of the Bible. And because it draws on the Bible, the story sounds "orthodox" and "traditional" to many mainstream Christians.[10] Whether this reading of the Bible is "really" Christian is a question for theologians, not sociologists. But as we will see, this deep story is not only widespread, it is also centuries old.

The people who wove this story together—the scriptwriters if you will—are not fringe figures either. On the contrary, they have included—and still do—famous Christian preachers, writers, and laypeople who were squarely within the mainstream of their times.[11] Which is why white Christian nationalism still flows along undisturbed in many regions of mainstream Christianity even today.

But that is not the only place where it can be found. White Christian nationalism has also shaped American popular culture. Consider the "post-apocalyptic" genre of novels and movies, such as "The Road." Or superhero comics and films, such as "Captain America." Today, the secularized version of white Christian nationalism is almost as important as the religious one. Though sometimes it is hard to distinguish between the two, as evidenced by the many cosplay crusaders among the Capitol insurrectionists and the overlaps between Christian "prophecy belief" and the "QAnon" conspiracy theory.[12]

But white Christian nationalism is not just a deep story about what was; it is also a political vision of what should be. First and foremost, of course, white Christian nationalists believe that America should be a Christian nation, or, at least, a nation ruled by Christians. And though the expectation of "whiteness" is rarely expressed explicitly, it is often clearly assumed in the sort of "Christian" that adherents of white Christian nationalism have in mind. Who counts as "white" and what counts as "Christian" has changed over time. White Christian nationalism's enemies have also changed, from Native Americans and Catholics, to communists, Black radicals, atheists, Muslims, and socialists, each taking their turn as the main threat to "(white) Christian values."

But there is more to the political vision than that. As we will show in the chapters ahead, contemporary proponents of white Christian nationalism also hold strong views on many other issues, including racial discrimination, religious freedom, government regulation, socialism, the welfare state, COVID lockdowns, voting, and the Capitol insurrection. Some of these views seem at odds with each other. Why would someone strongly favor institutionalizing Christianity as the national religion but also claim that one of their top priorities is "religious freedom"? Why would someone strongly affirm that the government should "advocate Christian values" and yet support the use of torture or oppose gun regulations? And many of them don't have an obvious connection to Christianity at all. There is no Commandment saying, "Thou shalt not wear a mask."

What connects these stances to each other is a particular understanding of freedom, order, and violence with deep roots in American history.[13] Freedom is understood in a libertarian way, as freedom from restrictions, especially by the government. Order is understood in a hierarchical way, with white Christian men at the top. And violence is seen as a righteous means of defending freedom and restoring order, means that are reserved to white Christian men. This understanding of freedom, order, and violence is the heart of white Christian nationalism.

We can now start to see how the various pieces of the political vision fit together. Government regulation infringes on the freedom of white Christians. So do mask mandates and COVID lockdowns. "Urban crime" and "racial riots" threaten the social order. They must be met with force by the police or, barring that, by good Christian men. Thus, the need for access to firearms. The general principle is this: white men must sometimes exercise righteous violence to defend (their) freedom and maintain social (and racial) order. It is freedom for "us" and authoritarian social order for "them."

This "us vs. them" tribalism may seem un-Christian, the glorification of violence even more so. But not if seen through the lens of the end times theology we mentioned earlier, with its sharp division between a good "us" and "evil" them, and its gory tales of "spiritual warfare." The goal is to forever redeem and restore a lost world corrupted by "outsiders." That won't happen without a fight. So, white Christian nationalism marches its adherents toward a bloody battle. This "ethno-traditionalist" impulse of white Christian nationalism is one of the things driving the authoritarian populism that has overwhelmed our cultural and political landscape in the last decade. It's why the highly regimented culture wars of the late 20th century have given way to the chaotic culture fights of the early 21st century.[14]

Demographic change is also a key factor. As white Christians approach minority status, white Christian nationalists are starting to turn against American democracy. After all, the basic principle of democratic government is majority rule. So long as white Christians were in the majority and could call the shots, they were willing to tolerate a certain amount of pluralism, provided that "minorities" did not insist too much on equality. Now faced with the prospect of minority status themselves, some members of the old white majority are embracing authoritarian politics as a means of protecting their "freedom."[15]

Is their freedom really in danger? They surely believe that it is. White Christian nationalists sincerely believe that whites and Christians are the most persecuted groups in America.[16] Consequently they view efforts to expand access to the democratic process—such as removing obstacles to voter participation—as an existential threat to their political power.

The United States cannot be both a truly multiracial democracy—a people of people and a nation of nations—and a white Christian nation at the same time. This is why white Christian nationalism has become a serious threat to American democracy, perhaps the most serious threat it now faces.

Before saying more about what white Christian nationalism *is*, it's important to make clear what it *is not*.

First, white Christian nationalism is not "Christian patriotism." White Christian nationalism idealizes the power of white Christian Americans. It is rooted in white supremacist assumptions and empowered by anger and fear. This is nationalism, not patriotism.

Patriotism, as the political philosopher Steven Smith explains, is first and foremost "loyalty . . . to one's constitution or political regime." Nationalism is loyalty to one's tribe "but always at the expense of an outgroup, who are deemed un-American, traitors, and enemies of the people." One reason the two sometimes get confused, as historian Jill Lepore explains, is that nationalism often disguises itself as patriotism: "Because it's difficult to convince people to pursue a course of aggression, violence, and domination . . . nationalists pretend their aims are instead protection and unity and that their motivation is patriotism. This is a lie. Patriotism is animated by love, nationalism by hatred. To confuse the one for the other is to pretend that hate is love and fear is courage."[17]

Is it possible for a Christian to be a patriot? Certainly.[18] So long as patriotism is understood in terms of constitutional ideals and democratic institutions and citizenship is not based on racial, ethnic, or religious identity. But if you pledge allegiance to your own ethno-cultural tribe, and place them above the rights of your fellow citizens, then you have crossed the line into white Christian nationalism.

Second, white Christian nationalism is not synonymous with white evangelicalism per se, even if there is considerable overlap. Though we may not be able to say that for much longer, as white evangelicalism becomes more and more synonymous with Republican voting and reactionary politics. To be sure, some evangelical leaders publicly distanced themselves from Trump in 2016. Others did so later. But many others not only supported Trump that year; they doubled down on Trump in 2020, arguing that he'd kept his promises to defend religious liberty and appoint conservative justices. Still others, such as Southern Baptist Theological Seminary President Al Mohler, had a born-again experience in the interim. In 2016, Mohler had promised that he would "Never. Ever.

Period." vote for Trump.[19] By 2020, he'd seen the light on his road to Damascus. So did the people in the pews: white evangelical support for Trump actually *increased* between 2016 and 2020.[20]

There is another reason why white Christian nationalism isn't synonymous with white evangelicalism though: it has many non-evangelical supporters, including a significant number of mainline Protestants; white Roman Catholics; and, even more, white Pentecostals. Yet another reason is that a minority of white evangelicals are actively resisting white Christian nationalism. Indeed, following the events of January 6, 2021, the faculty of Wheaton College—the "evangelical Harvard"—released a formal statement condemning the insurrection and denouncing "Christian nationalism" and "white supremacism." These counter-currents give some measure of hope that the subculture of white evangelicalism may yet be reformed from within.[21]

Third and finally, white Christian nationalism is not just a problem among white American *Christians*. There are secular versions of white Christian nationalism that claim to defend "Western Culture" or "Judeo-Christian civilization." And there are secular white Americans who know how to leverage white Christian nationalist language. For such Americans, the "Christian" label simply signals shared tribal identity or veils political values that would otherwise be socially unacceptable. That is certainly how Trump himself used the label—as a rallying cry and a fig leaf—and one reason why so many white Christians have been attracted to him: not because he himself is an exemplar of Christian piety, but because he waved the Christian flag and announced his willingness to "fight" for it.

For some white Christian nationalists, the fight has become more important than the faith. This is one reason why many leaders on the Christian right were so unexcited about the prospect of a Pence presidency during Trump's first impeachment, despite Pence's unimpeachable evangelical credentials: Pence had the faith, but Trump had the fight, and it was the fight they really cared about. That is because their goal is power, not piety. Nor was this the first time they prioritized fighting over faith. Remember that in the 2016 primaries a majority of white conservative Christians chose Trump over numerous GOP candidates with far stronger evangelical bona fides. They wanted a fighter *for* Christians (read: people like us), not someone who fights *like a* Christian.[22]

This merger of religious nationalism and white nationalism is hardly unique to the United States. In Europe and Latin America, there is a secularized version of Christian nationalism whose central tenet is the defense of "white culture," "Christian Civilization," and a "traditional way of life." Something similar seems to be emerging in the United States. In this regard, as in many others, America is unexceptional.[23] Ironically, the more some conservatives insist on "American exceptionalism," the less exceptional it becomes.

Now, for a brief preview of what follows.

Chapter 1 addresses the "what" question and also the "who" question. It uses survey data to "operationalize" white Christian nationalism: that is, to define, measure, and assess its effects. Chapter 2 addresses the "when" question and also the "why" question. It uses historical evidence to show when and why the white Christian nationalist version of American history took shape and also how it has changed over time. Chapter 3 takes up the "how" question in the sense of "how does it work in contemporary American politics?" The conclusion takes up the "where" question: Where is all this headed, and how do we make sure the answer is not "off a cliff."

The only way to avert that outcome is to build a popular front in defense of American democracy, an alliance that extends from #NeverTrump Republicans to Democratic Socialists, an alliance that includes religious conservatives as well as secular progressives. Building that alliance will not be easy. Christian leaders will have to convince at least some of their followers that white Christian nationalism is neither "Biblical" nor "patriotic," but idolatrous and un-Christian. And progressive leaders will have to be willing to join hands with them. There are moments when political principles are more important than policy debates. This is one of them.

# Chapter 1

# "This Is Our Nation, Not Theirs"

Survey all the rioters who've been rounded up since the attempted insurrection on January 6, 2021, and it's unlikely that many would describe themselves as "Christian nationalists" let alone "*white* Christian nationalists." Even the overtly Christian ones—the guy carrying a "Jesus saves" sign, or waving a Christian flag, or saying a prayer in Jesus's name on the Senate floor—would probably reject these labels. Nor would many (if any) admit to being "white nationalists," "conspiracy theorists," "insurrectionists," "white supremacists," or any other label with such obviously negative connotations.

In interviews, most of the rioters have described themselves as something like "Christian patriots." In his prayer on the Senate floor, for example, the so-called QAnon Shaman described his fellow insurrectionists as "patriots that love [God] and that love Christ," defending "the American way" from "the tyrants, the communists, and the globalists" as well as "the traitors within our government," sending a message that "this is our nation, not theirs."[1] And if even the insurrectionists wouldn't identify as white Christian nationalists, then we can be fairly certain most white conservative Christians would take offense at the label.

So, are we just peddling a slur? Are we throwing around a menacing name to demonize people with whom we disagree? Are we weaponizing vague buzzwords to silence conservative Christians who are just standing up for their values? Are we just mimicking reactionary leaders who smear progressives as "godless socialists" preaching "critical race theory" to the congregation of "wokeness"?

To each question, we answer "no." We aim to define our terms carefully and back up our argument empirically.

We define white Christian national*ism* and identify white Christian national*ists* using a constellation of beliefs. These are beliefs that, we argue, reflect a desire to restore and privilege the myths, values, identity, and authority of a particular ethnocultural tribe. These beliefs add up to a political vision that privileges that tribe. And they seek to put other tribes in their "proper" place.

White Christian nationalism is *nationalist* because it rejects pluralism and what many on the right call "globalism." It expresses a desire for national unity and international power. But unity around what? And power for whom? Unity around what political scientist Eric Kaufmann calls "ethno-traditionalism," a national myth that blurs distinctions between culture and race with talk of "Christian heritage and values."[2] And power for whites. Because when some whites—many whites, in fact—hear the words "Christian" and "American," they think of "people who look and think like us." A *truly* Christian nation, in their view, would celebrate and privilege the sacred history, liberty, and rightful rule of white conservatives, tolerating "others" at best; enslaving, expelling, or exterminating them at worst. This is the root of the massive resistance of some whites to removing Confederate statues or to teaching about racism in American history—to impugn the racial history of the nation is to dispute the chosenness and fundamental goodness of white Christians.

When the QAnon Shaman thanked his Heavenly Father for "allowing us to send a message ... that this is our nation, not theirs," he was also issuing a warning: they were ready to use violence to take back "their" country. Far from being an empty smear or a slur against white religious conservatives, what we call "white Christian nationalism" represents a serious threat—a threat to American democracy, itself.

## WHAT'S *CHRISTIAN* ABOUT CHRISTIAN NATIONALISM?

In the next chapter we look at how the deep story of white Christian nationalism first came together and how it has evolved and changed over time. But first, in this chapter, we use survey data to document the political vision of white Christian nationalism and quantify its reach in contemporary America. We'll mostly use data we collected ourselves in a nationally representative survey over multiple waves from 2019 through 2021. And we'll occasionally supplement with reference to other sources.[3]

We use seven different indicators of Christian nationalism. Often, we'll combine them together, but sometimes we use them in different combinations depending on which measures we have available. Each measure is a question asking Americans to indicate their level of agreement with various statements.

1. "I consider founding documents like the Declaration of Independence and the US Constitution to be divinely inspired."
2. "The success of the United States is part of God's plan."

3. "The federal government should declare the United States a Christian nation."
4. "The federal government should advocate Christian values."
5. "The federal government should enforce a strict separation of church and state."
6. "The federal government should allow the display of religious symbols in public spaces."
7. "The federal government should allow prayer in public schools."

When understood in the context of American religious and political history, each indicator tells us something about how Americans perceive the connection between Christianity and American civic life. Americans who agree at some level with the first two statements are affirming that God "inspired" the nation's founding documents and that God has somehow orchestrated America's prosperity and perhaps will do so in the future. At minimum, both statements imply that God has a special relationship with the United States.

The remaining five statements ask Americans to affirm what they think the government *should* do, reflecting their political theology. Formally declaring the United States a "Christian nation" would be the most explicit declaration of Christian nationalism. But also, believing the government should "advocate Christian values" at the very least indicates Americans think "Christian values" (whatever they may understand by that term) are worthwhile for the government to promote as policy. And regarding the "separation of church and state," we pay attention to Americans who *disagree* with that statement, indicating they want church and state to have a closer relationship.

The last two statements may sound more innocuous. But both statements actually reference more explicit historical debates.

For example, the statement about religious symbols represents long-standing legal debates involving things like placing the Ten Commandments in courthouses or using crosses on state seals. And the last statement about prayer references a decades-long disagreement about earlier Supreme Court decisions prohibiting teacher-led prayer and Bible reading in public schools. In other words, while references to "religious symbols" or "prayer" in public spaces may sound rather harmless, they evoke contentious political debates.

Throughout the book we'll combine responses to make a "Christian nationalism scale" ranging from 0–28 or 0–24 (The difference is because the question about the founding documents being divinely inspired hasn't been asked in every survey).

Where is Christian nationalism most prevalent in the American population? While previous books have focused on a variety of religious and demographic characteristics associated with this ideology, here we pay closer attention to differences among Christian groups that cut across racial categories.[4] This is where the "whiteness" of white Christian nationalism will come into play. As we'll see, the link that connects the deep story and political vision of Christian nationalism is whiteness. When that link is missing, as it is among Black Americans who score high on our Christian nationalism measure, the connection to the political vision is broken.

Figure 1.1 presents average scores across two categories: narrower denominational groupings (e.g., Pentecostals or Baptists, in Panel A) and broader ethno-religious traditions (e.g., white evangelicals, in Panel B). We've arranged the scores from lowest to highest, starting from the left. Several findings immediately jump out. Among denominational groupings, theologically conservative Protestant groups score the highest, with those in the Pentecostal, Holiness, and Baptist traditions leading the way. Nondenominational Protestants, as political scientists like Ryan

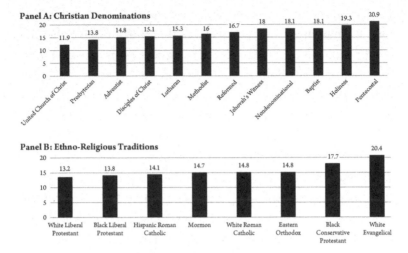

Figure 1.1. Average Christian Nationalism Score across Narrow and Broad Christian Traditions.

**Note:** Possible scores ranged 0–28. The labels "Evangelical," "Conservative," and "Liberal" are determined in response to a question about whether respondents consider themselves "born again or evangelical Christians." Those who answered yes are considered evangelical or conservative, while those who answered no are considered more theologically "liberal."

**Source:** *Public Discourse and Ethics Survey (Wave 7; February 2021)*

Burge and Paul Djupe have pointed out, are overwhelmingly evangelical in their leanings.[5] Mainline traditions tend to score lower on Christian nationalist ideology, likely reflecting both their theological and political liberalism compared to groups like Pentecostals and Baptists.[6]

In terms of broader ethno-religious traditions, white evangelicals unsurprisingly score the highest of all groups, with more liberal white Protestants scoring the lowest. Most other broad traditions including Eastern Orthodox Christians, Mormons, white and Hispanic Roman Catholics, and Black liberal Protestants score similarly to the white liberal Protestants.

Surprisingly, Black conservative Protestants score closer to white evangelicals than to Black liberal Protestants. Does this finding contradict our argument that Christian nationalism is connected to white racial identity and even white supremacy? Not when we understand what religious language means in its political and historical context.

## AMERICA'S MOST EFFECTIVE DOG WHISTLE

In her 2021 *Christian Post* article, "The Assault on 'White America,'" Hedieh Mirahmadi writes, "[W]e must acknowledge the widespread assault on the conservative Christian community. I use the phrase 'White America,' though ironically we are comprised of all ethnicities and races but united in our stand for biblical and democratic values that are the foundation of our country."[7] Notice what the author is assuming. She states that conservative Christians are under attack, but she takes this as an assault on *white* America." She even acknowledges that the group under attack comprises multiple races and ethnicities, but what makes them "white" apparently is their united stand for America's foundational biblical and democratic values. Mirahmadi's rhetorical sleight-of-hand is not unusual. White Christian nationalists often use religion to hide race in this way. But it is a little clumsy. She gives away the game too easily.

White Christian nationalists did not always need to play this game though. Before the civil rights movement, white politicians who wanted to stir up their voters could just use racial slurs. After the civil rights movement, they had to find more subtle ways of invoking race. They invented code words that triggered the racial anxieties of white voters. On his deathbed, Republican strategist Lee Atwater confessed that when openly saying the N-word started to backfire and hurt politicians, he urged Nixon to adopt the language of "states' rights" and "forced bussing." Later, Reagan would use phrases like "welfare queen" and "bucks" to vilify poor Blacks. More recent formulations included "super-predator," "thugs," "illegals," and "terrorists." Similarly, words like "communist" and "socialist" have been racially coded since the "red scares" of the 1920s and even more so since the civil rights movement of the 1960s. Martin Luther King Jr. was often vilified as a "communist."[8] Like a high-pitched whistle that can only be heard by a dog, the code words were uniquely effective for those with prejudiced ears.

Dog whistles can be used to signal "us" as well as "them." Since the Reagan era, white conservative Christianity has become increasingly synonymous with Republican politics and identity. As a result, the word "Christian" has increasingly taken on racial connotations in the minds of conservative whites. Even seemingly race-neutral phrases like "Christian heritage" or "Christian worldview" or "Christian values" now imply "conservative *white* values."

How do we know this? Remember the indicators we use to measure Christian nationalism say absolutely nothing about race or ethnicity. So, whether someone agrees or disagrees with those statements should tell us very little about their racial attitudes, right? But if you're a white American, they absolutely do.

Figure 1.2 shows how Black and white Americans score on a question about how much they think white and Black Americans will experience discrimination in the next year. We asked this question in February 2021, after Joe Biden had taken office. Lower scores indicate that respondents think whites or Blacks won't experience much discrimination. We used a statistical model that allows us to track Americans' responses while holding constant the influences of political party, political conservatism, religious characteristics, and other sociodemographic factors. We then plotted how the predicted values change across respondents' average scores on our full Christian nationalism scale.

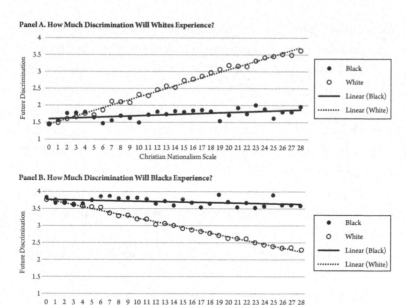

Panel A. How Much Discrimination Will Whites Experience?

Panel B. How Much Discrimination Will Blacks Experience?

Figure 1.2. White and Black Americans indicating how much discrimination they think whites/Blacks will experience within the next year across Christian nationalism.

*Note:* Y-axis values: 1 = None at all; 2 = A little; 3 = Some; 4 = A lot. Ordinary least squares regression models including full Christian nationalism scale, political party identification, political conservatism, religious tradition, religiosity, age, gender, race, educational attainment, income, and region of the country. Significant interaction term between Christian nationalism × Black ($p < .01$).

*Source:* *Public Discourse and Ethics Survey (Wave 7; February 2021)*

Look at Panel A first. The trend for Black Americans is essentially flat. What they think about America's relationship to Christianity has basically no influence on their belief that white Americans will experience relatively little discrimination in the next year. Now look at white Americans. The higher white Americans score on our Christian nationalism scale, the more discrimination they believe whites will experience within the next year. And the trend is highly linear, meaning that, for whites, Christian nationalism and belief in anti-white discrimination increase in lockstep with one another.

Panel B asks about how much discrimination respondents think Black Americans will experience in the next year. We now see a mirror image of the first pattern. Regardless of what Black Americans think about the place of Christianity in American politics, their belief that Black Americans will face some discrimination starts high and stays high. But for white Americans, the more strongly they adhere to Christian nationalism, the less likely they are to think Black Americans will face much discrimination at all. And here again, the association is highly linear.

How do we explain these divergent patterns? Is it because our Christian nationalism measure is really just measuring Republican identification or a conservative political orientation? No. Remember that we held those factors constant in our statistical model, along with religious tradition and commitment, age, education, and even region of the country. In fact, these same patterns hold for most political issues we've asked about in our various surveys. Indicators of Christian nationalism (in combination or included separately) are powerful predictors of ultra-conservatism for white Americans, especially on any issues involving race, discrimination, xenophobia, or justice. But they have very little influence on the attitudes of Black Americans. And often little influence on Hispanic Americans too.[9] As noted earlier, whiteness is the hidden link that transforms the deep story of Christian nationalism into a political vision.

Is the era of dog whistle politics over? Perhaps. Though not in the way one might imagine. More and more, the quiet part is not just said out loud; it's shouted to the heavens. In July 2020, for example, evangelical activist Eric Metaxas tweeted, "Jesus was white. Did he have 'white privilege' even though he was without sin?" The statement was absurd on its face. The idea of a "white race" did not even exist in Jesus's time. But Metaxas's message was clear enough: "Jesus was one of us. He was part of our tribe."[21] And, like him, we are without (racial) sin.

Black Americans are more likely to draw a far different connection between Christianity and whiteness, both in the present and within our nation's history. As author James Baldwin famously wrote,

> The American Negro has the great advantage of having never believed the collection of myths to which white Americans cling: that their ancestors were all freedom-loving heroes, that they were born in the greatest country the world has ever seen, or that Americans are invincible in battle and wise in peace, that Americans have always dealt honorably with Mexicans and Indians and all other neighbors or inferiors.[10]

Baldwin explained that the white Americans who held these myths were "the slightly mad victims of their own brainwashing." Fifty years on, Baldwin's words still ring truer than many white Americans want to believe.

Christian pastors and politicians have played a central role in crafting and disseminating these myths. In his 2003 book, *What if America Were a Christian Nation Again?*, for example, the late pastor D. James Kennedy wrote that the "nation was founded by the Pilgrims and the Puritans," and that "As late as 1775, 98 percent of the people were [evangelicals]." Former Speaker of the House and author of *Rediscovering God in America* Newt Gingrich once said on *Meet the Press*, "most people don't realize it's illegal to pray" in public schools. And former Governor of Alaska Sarah Palin once explained to Bill O'Reilly why "America is a Christian nation," claiming, "You can just go to our Founding Fathers' early documents and see how they crafted a Declaration of Independence and a Constitution that allows that Judeo-Christian belief to be the foundation of our lives." And she concludes the founding documents are "quite clear that we would create law based on the God of the Bible and the Ten Commandments."[11]

And these *are* myths: the United States was not founded by Pilgrims and Puritans. Ninety-eight percent of America's inhabitants were not "evangelicals" at the founding. It has never been illegal to pray in public school. And the Constitution says absolutely nothing about God, the Bible, or the Ten Commandments.

Nor is this just a difference in "worldview." It's not that Christian nationalists have a different understanding of American history; it's that they often have an *incorrect* understanding. But only if they are white. In one of our surveys, we gave respondents a short quiz that included five true/false statements about religion in American political history.

1. The 1st Amendment says Congress can't restrict religious liberty, but Congress could make laws privileging Christianity. (False)
2. The U.S. Constitution references our country's obligations to God several times. (False)
3. The phrase "In God We Trust" did not become the nation's official motto until after 1950. (True)
4. The phrase "under God" was not added to the pledge of allegiance until after 1950. (True)
5. Supreme Court decisions in the 1960s made it illegal for students to pray or read their Bibles in public schools. (False)

Respondents could answer true, false, or don't know. We then calculated the average percentage Americans got correct on the quiz.

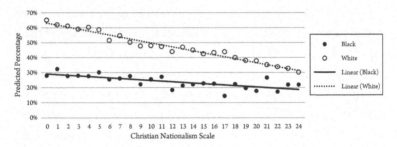

Figure 1.3. Average percentage correct on religion in American political history quiz by Christian nationalism and race.

**Note:** Ordinary least squares regression models including Christian nationalism scale, political party identification, political conservatism, religious tradition, religiosity, age, gender, race, educational attainment, income, and region of the country. Significant interaction term between Christian nationalism × Black (p < .05).

**Source:** *Public Discourse and Ethics Survey (Wave 4; August 2020)*

Figure 1.3 shows how scores change across adherence to Christian nationalism for both white and Black Americans. Black Americans tend to score lower than whites on the quiz, primarily because they are more likely to simply say they don't know. But there is no association between their scores on the test and their adherence to Christian nationalism. Not so with whites. The higher they score on Christian nationalism, the lower they score on the test. Why? Not because they don't give answers but because they give *wrong* answers.

Why are they so misinformed? In part, because there is a cottage industry that spreads historical misinformation. It includes amateur "historians" like David Barton and religious right organizations like Focus on the Family, WallBuilders, and even Donald Trump's 1776 Commission. But if historical misinformation were the whole story, we'd expect these incorrect views about religion's place in American political history to exhibit the same pattern among Black Americans. But they don't.

And research suggests this isn't just plain old ignorance, either. When scholars assess religious conservatives' knowledge of many aspects of science (for example, atoms, lasers, viruses, or genes), they score well. It is only when they are asked about hotly contested culture-war topics (for example, evolution or the Big Bang) that they do poorly. This is why white Americans who more strongly affirm that America should be for "people like us" are more likely to answer questions about religion in America's political history in a way that elevates the preeminence and alleged persecution of Christianity. Not only may they have learned erroneous religious history, but the ideology of white Christian nationalism may incline white Americans to *re*interpret their history in ways that elevate their own group as heroes and victims.

We can see this sort of ideologically driven approach to history more directly when we see how Christian nationalism corresponds to whites' views about the Civil War and Confederate monuments. In August 2020, we asked Americans if they believed "historians debate whether slavery was a central cause of the Civil War" (an issue that is frankly of virtually no dispute among historians). We also asked them whether they would support the removal of Confederate monuments and statues of former slave owners—the vast majority of which were erected in the early 1900s to valorize the antebellum South—because of their racist legacy (see Figure 1.4). Even after holding other relevant characteristics constant, as white Americans more strongly affirm the centrality of Christianity to American civic life, the more likely they are to question the centrality of slavery to the Civil War and to oppose removing monuments to America's white supremacist past.

Knowing these patterns help us understand that white Christian nationalism is not just a set of conscious (if erroneous) beliefs about America's past. It is also a set of unconscious desires about America's

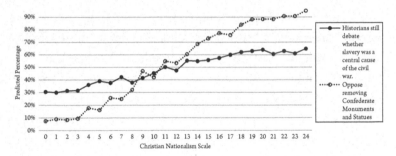

Figure 1.4. Predicted percentage of white Americans who question slavery's centrality to the Civil War and oppose removing Confederate monuments and statues across Christian nationalism.

**Note:** Binary logistic regression models including Christian nationalism scale, political party identification, political conservatism, religious tradition, religiosity, age, gender, educational attainment, income, and region of the country. **Source:** *Public Discourse and Ethics (Wave 4; August 2020).*

future. Our measures tap into how much Americans think the government *should* formally recognize the nation's "Christian" identity or advocate "Christian values." When we understand these as racialized terms, we can understand why white Americans who favor institutionalizing "Christianity" in American politics would fear that *whites* specifically will be threatened under a Democratic president. And why they worry Blacks will be given special treatment.

This is why we must be specific that the phenomenon we're describing in this book is *white* Christian nationalism. At issue is not just religious nostalgia or even religious conservatism, as if such things transcended ethnic and racial identities. Rather, it is an acute strain of ethno-traditionalism in which "white" and "Christian" are conflated into a single identity—"white-Christian."

Dog whistles are effective to the extent that the target population hears and understands their intended meaning, while most others remain oblivious. Even as it's become riskier for mainstream politicians to use negative dog whistles like "thug" or "welfare queen," the word "Christian" remains the right's most effective signal to white conservatives that "our values," "our heritage," "our way of life," and "our influence" are under attack, and "we" must respond. Christianity and American-ness are both raced.

But what sort of response does the ethno-traditionalism of white Christian nationalism provoke among whites? The characteristics we link with white Christian nationalism could all be considered components of what's commonly called "populism," an orientation or ideology that pits corrupt "elites" against virtuous common folk. Its components are, among other things, scapegoating of minorities; distrust in science, the media, and "establishment" politicians; corresponding trust in strongman leaders; and conspiratorial thinking. White Christian nationalism unites all these elements. As a result, it is one of the strongest currents within American right-wing populism and one of the main drivers of political polarization.

Can that polarization be overcome?

## WHY DIDN'T "THE ASTEROID" OF COVID-19 UNITE US?

Moral psychologist Jonathan Haidt has become one of America's leading sources for understanding political polarization. His 2012 bestseller, *The Righteous Mind: Why Good People Are Divided by Politics and Religion*, presciently described the intensifying polarization that was both a cause and an effect of the Trump presidency. In the end, however, even Haidt's diagnosis proved too sanguine. In a popular TED Talk that accompanied the 2012 book, Haidt mused that a common threat might restore common ground in American politics. If Americans learned that a large asteroid was on course to strike earth within a few years, he speculated, they would surely throw aside their petty differences and come together to strategize, coordinate, and sacrifice so that humanity could survive.

And then that asteroid arrived in the form of COVID-19. And Americans did not come together. Instead they became more polarized than ever. To be sure, consistent information about how to stop the spread of COVID-19 was difficult to pin down during the first few months of 2020. But familiar fissures emerged in answers to questions like the following: Who is to blame? Whom do we trust? And what should we do? The populist impulse stoked by white Christian nationalism shaped answers to all three questions.

In the early months of the COVID-19 outbreak in the United States, the media subjected President Trump to harsh criticism for minimizing the threat of the virus. As infections and deaths started to spiral upward, Trump and his allies sought to deflect the blame. As so often in American history, racial minorities were scapegoated. In this case, it was Chinese Americans and immigrants. It still is. Republican politicians and pundits such as Florida Gov. Ron De Santis and Fox News commentator Tucker Carlson were quick to blame the Delta variant on "illegal immigrants" crossing the Southern border.

Trump and many of his Republican surrogates or supporters repeatedly referred to the coronavirus as "the China Virus" or "the Kung-Flu" and suggested that the virus had either escaped or been deliberately released from a Chinese lab. In other words, the Trump administration was not to blame for the virus; China was. Trump would use the expression "Chinese virus" more than 20 times just in the latter half of March. A photographer snapped a picture of Trump's notes for speech in which he'd crossed out the word "Corona" and inserted "Chinese." Other times, Christian nationalist commentators curiously accused Mexican immigrants of worsening the pandemic, despite the fact that Mexico had still been largely untouched by COVID-19 at that time. On March 10, 2020, when Mexico had seven total reported cases of COVID-19, Charlie Kirk, founder and president of Turning Point USA and former director of the now-defunct Falkirk Center at Liberty University, tweeted that "Now, more than ever, we need the wall. With China Virus spreading across the globe, the US stands a chance if we can control of [sic] our borders." Trump reposted the tweet and added the comment, "Going up fast. We need the Wall more than ever."

In May 2020, we asked Americans various questions related to race, immigration, and the pandemic. The responses were telling (see Figure 1.5). Our models took into account various factors that might lead white Americans to support Trump's narrative scapegoating China, the Chinese, or Mexican immigrants such as conservative ideology, Republican identification, or education. Even after holding such factors constant, we found that as adherence to Christian nationalism increased, whites were more likely to feel that our lax immigration laws were partly to blame for the pandemic, to

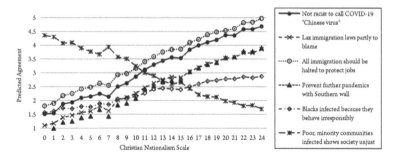

Figure 1.5. White Americans' predicted agreement with questions connecting race and immigration to the COVID-19 pandemic across Christian nationalism. **Note:** Ordinary least squares regression models including Christian nationalism scale, political party identification, political conservatism, religious tradition, religiosity, age, gender, educational attainment, income, and region of the country.
**Source:** *Public Discourse and Ethics Survey (Wave 3; May 2020)*

believe that immigration should be halted to protect American jobs, that we could thwart future pandemics by building the southern border wall, and that it wasn't racist to call COVID-19 "the Chinese virus."

But white Christian nationalism wasn't just associated with blaming minorities *outside* of the country. It was also linked with whites blaming minorities *inside* the country for their dispropor-tionate infection rates. Early on in the pandemic it became clear that poorer, minority communities were being infected with COVID-19 at higher rates. Public health scholars determined this was largely due to the fact that poorer minorities were more likely to work in situations where they couldn't safely distance (e.g., food service), have comorbidities, and live in areas with less access to health care.[12] However, we asked Americans how much they agreed with statements placing the blame for higher infection rates on Black Americans behaving irresponsibly or, conversely, on our unjust society (see Figure 1.5). As we might expect, the more that white Americans affirmed Christian nationalism, the more likely they were to blame Blacks themselves and disagree that their higher infection rates were a symptom of circumstance. These patterns make little sense unless we remember that, for whites, political theology also reflects racialized assumptions about civic belonging and worth.[13]

But because white Christian nationalism is ultimately about "us" (the good, decent Americans) versus "them" (the outsiders who wish to take what's rightfully ours), it also shaped who Americans trusted for information during the pandemic. In the same May 2020 survey, we provided a list of entities including Donald Trump, Republicans, Congress, religious communities, scientists, the Center for Disease Control (CDC), and other sources. We then asked respondents how much they trusted each group for information regarding COVID-19. Figure 1.6 shows the predicted percentage of white Americans

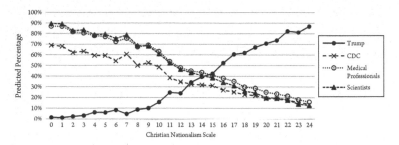

Figure 1.6. Predicted percentage of white Americans who express "a great deal" of trust in experts or Donald Trump during COVID-19 across Christian nationalism.

**Note:** Binary logistic regression models including Christian nationalism scale, political party identification, political conservatism, religious tradition, religiosity, age, gender, educational attainment, income, and region of the country.

**Source:** *Public Discourse and Ethics Survey (Wave 3; May 2020)*

who trusted experts such as the CDC, medical professionals, or scientists, or Donald Trump "a great deal." We plot the averages across whites' adherence to Christian nationalism.

The differences are striking. Even after accounting for religious, political, and sociodemographic characteristics, as Christian nationalism increases, white Americans' confidence in each expert group starts high and declines precipitously. And just the opposite for Trump. As Christian nationalism increases, trust for Donald Trump soars. The end result is that at extremely high levels of Christian nationalism, less than 20% of white Americans expressed "a great deal" of trust in experts, while over 85% reported a great deal of trust in Donald Trump.

Predictably, given the enormous trust white Christian nationalists place in Trump, we see a corresponding distrust in mainstream news media among white Americans who score higher on Christian nationalism. All presidents have complicated relationships with the free press. And this is how it should be. In democracies, the press should be able to call "balls and strikes" on political leaders, fact-checking false claims and reporting on the real-world consequences of failed policies. But like no other president since Nixon, Donald Trump has famously excoriated "lamestream" news outlets as "fake news," both leveraging and fueling populist distrust in mainstream media. His feud continued unabated during the pandemic. On February 26, 2020, for example, Trump tweeted, "Low Ratings Fake News MSDNC (Comcast) & CNN are doing everything possible to make the Caronavirus [sic] look as bad as possible, including panicking markets, if possible. Likewise their incompetent Do Nothing Democrat comrades are all talk, no action. USA in great shape!"

In this and other tweets, Trump assures his followers that media are actively working in cooperation with Democrats to exaggerate the threat of COVID-19, hoping to tank markets and make him look bad. It should be little surprise then, that when we asked Americans in May 2020 how much they trusted 10 different news sources, among white Americans, overall trust in all news outlets plummeted as their adherence to Christian nationalism increased. There were only two exceptions: Fox News and Breitbart. As Christian nationalism increased, white Americans' trust in either of these news sources took off.

With such disparities in trust in medical experts and mainstream news, it comes as no surprise that white Christian nationalism powerfully predicted resistance to following the recommendations of health experts publicized through most news outlets during the early stages of the pandemic. When we asked Americans in May 2020 how frequently they followed recommended precautions for limiting the spread of COVID-19 such as wearing a mask in public or washing hands more frequently, white Americans who scored higher on Christian nationalism were much less likely to take such precautions. In fact, they were more likely to engage in behavior that experts discouraged, such as meeting with large numbers of people, eating out in restaurants, or going shopping for nonessentials.[14]

These patterns have repeated themselves when it comes to COVID vaccine resistance. Polls taken in late 2020 and early 2021 found that white evangelical Protestants were the group most likely to say they didn't plan on taking the COVID-19 vaccine when it became available. While most journalists and scholars were quickly able to point out the combination of distrust and ignorance behind these patterns, few recognized the role of white Christian nationalism among the evangelical population. As we show in Figure 1.7, even after we account for other relevant factors in statistical models, in February 2021 only roughly 5% of white Americans who score the lowest on our full Christian nationalism scale indicated that they wouldn't get vaccinated. That percentage steadily climbs to 50% at the highest levels of Christian nationalism. By contrast, over 85% of white Americans who largely reject Christian nationalism

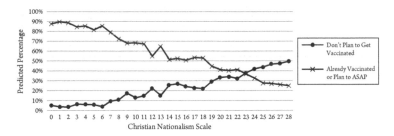

Figure 1.7. Predicted percentage of white Americans by COVID vaccine status across Christian nationalism.

**Note:** Binary logistic regression models including Christian nationalism scale, political party identification, political conservatism, religious tradition, religiosity, age, gender, educational attainment, income, and region of the country.

**Source:** *Public Discourse and Ethics Survey (Wave 7; February 2021)*

indicated they'd either already been vaccinated by February 2021 or would do so as soon as possible. That percentage declined in a linear fashion to less than 30% among the most ardent supporters of Christian nationalist ideology.[15]

Part of Trump's resistance to the recommendations of experts, and specifically shutting down businesses and mandating shelter-in-place orders, involved the potential consequences for the economy. On multiple occasions, Trump repeated the phrase, "The cure cannot be worse than the disease," stressing that it would ultimately be more damaging to keep the economy closed than to impose more restrictions in the hope of stopping the spread of the virus. At a White House press briefing in March 2020, Trump said decisions on how to handle the pandemic couldn't be left to medical experts: "If it were up to doctors, they may say, 'Let's shut down the entire world.' You know, we can't do that." Right-wing pundits made similar statements on air or over social media. Fox News host Laura Ingraham said, "Doctors provide medical treatment and cures—they should not be the determinative voices in policy making." Similarly, Charlie Kirk resented that, "The question we're not allowed to ask . . . is should the number of people who get sick be the only variable we factor into our ethical calculation? It's also impossible to dispute that the steps we are taking are destroying the American economy." And overtly Christian nationalist pastor Lance Wallnau went even further to argue tanking the economy was the Democrats' whole ballgame: "The virus will touch just a fraction of the population," he explained, "The Left wants the economy distressed because the crisis improves their chances of taking office."

Other Trump supporters on the Christian right emphasized the threat to personal liberty posed by mask mandates and lockdown restrictions. Former Arkansas governor and Baptist minister Mike Huckabee, for example, said in mid-April 2020 that lockdown enforcement was threatening Americans' "civil liberties" and effectively "shredding the Constitution." So too, pastor John MacArthur, who drew national criticism for reopening his megachurch during the pandemic and discouraging mask use, warned, "[J]ust terrify people that they might die and they'll all roll over in complete compliance. They'll give up their freedoms, they'll put on silly masks . . . they'll sit in their house for as long as you tell them to sit there. You can conquer an entire nation in fear."

This resistance from Trump and others isn't just the mindset of small-government, free-market conservatives who valorize free choice and prosperity as the panacea for society's ills. It's closely connected with white Christian nationalism. We'll discuss this connection more in a moment, but for now we can see the link clearly in how white Christian nationalism shaped whites' responses to mandated COVID-19 lockdowns and social distancing orders (see Figure 1.8). The more strongly white

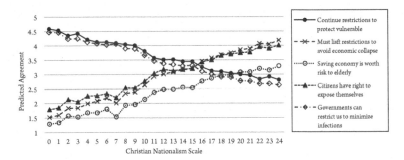

Figure 1.8. White Americans' predicted agreement with statements prioritizing the economy, personal liberty, or the vulnerable in considering COVID-19 lockdowns across Christian nationalism.

*Note:* Ordinary least squares regression models including Christian nationalism scale, political party identification, political conservatism, religious tradition, religiosity, age, gender, educational attainment, income, and region of the country.

*Source: Public Discourse and Ethics Survey (Wave 3; May 2020)*

Americans affirm Christian nationalism, the more likely they were to agree with statements stressing the need to protect individual liberty and the economy, even if it meant putting the elderly or the vulnerable at risk. Conversely, whites were less likely to prioritize the vulnerable the more they adhered to Christian nationalism.[16]

It is important to recognize how differently white Christian nationalism functions from "religious commitment" as social scientists traditionally measure it. As other studies have shown, white Christian nationalism and religious commitment are not the same, and often they move white Americans in different directions on issues of social justice and equality. In this case, white Christian nationalism goes in the opposite direction of religious commitment. That is to say, once we account for Christian nationalism in our statistical models, white Americans who attend church more often, pray more often, and consider religion more important are less likely to prioritize the economy or liberty over the vulnerable. Why is this the case? Because white Christian nationalism is about ethno-traditionalism and protecting the freedoms of a very narrowly defined "us." Religious commitment, in contrast, can expand what philosopher Peter Singer calls the "circle of empathy," our ability to put ourselves in others' shoes.

But if white Christian nationalism narrows our circle of empathy, there's another, closely connected ideology that helps justify *why* those outside the circle are so unworthy of help.

## THE *OTHER* DOG WHISTLE

For white Americans who affirm Christian nationalist ideology, "true Americans" aren't just natural-born white citizens who identify with conservative Christianity on, say, issues like abortion or transgender rights. Rather there is another aspect of what it means to be "truly American" that gets entangled in the conservative Christian identity: libertarian, free-market capitalism. We'll discuss the historical development and political impact of this strand of individualism extensively later. But here we want to introduce and demonstrate how they're connected empirically, influencing both the economic policies white Christian nationalism promotes and the groups white Christian nationalism fears the most. Unsurprisingly, we also find that the love affair between Christian nationalism and libertarian free-market capitalism is a racialized one, found most powerfully among white Americans.

In November 2020, we asked Americans a series of questions about economic systems and policies. We added up how much Americans agreed with statements like "Free markets are the key to our national prosperity" and "We must not over-regulate businesses or we will stifle productivity," along with others like "We need strong social safety nets to provide for those who cannot work," and "The government should intervene to reduce economic inequality" to create a scale. We ordered the responses such that higher scores tell us how strong of a free-market capitalist Americans were. When we ran statistical models to assess which factors predicted Americans' scores on the scale, we found that Christian nationalism was the second strongest factor in scoring higher, second only to political conservatism.

But what is just as interesting is that we found this connection between Christian nationalism and a strong preference for free-market ideals is exclusive to whites. Figure 1.9 shows the divergent patterns for white and Black Americans across Christian nationalism. As we've seen in previous figures, as scores on our Christian nationalism scale increase, Black Americans stay quite steady in

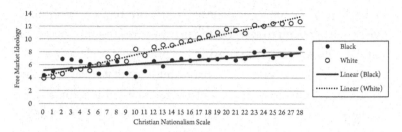

Figure 1.9. Predicted favorability toward free-market ideals by Christian nationalism and race.
*Note:* Ordinary least squares regression models including Christian nationalism scale, political party identification, political conservatism, religious tradition, religiosity, age, gender, race, educational attainment, income, and region of the country. Significant interaction term between Christian nationalism × Black (p = .001).
*Source: Public Discourse and Ethics Survey (Wave 6; November 2020)*

their approval of strong free-market attitudes. But white Americans increase tremendously in their support for markets unhindered by government intervention.

We should keep in mind that just as our Christian nationalism measures say nothing about race, neither do they mention anything about economics or markets. So why would we see such a powerful connection between Christian nationalism and a strong preference for unfettered capitalism? And why would this pattern be different for Black Americans?

There is a long history there that we'll unpack soon. But put simply, the idea of a "Christian nation," which was founded by people in favor of "our way of life" has not only become culturally inextricable from white Christian culture, but also from the "rugged individualism" that adherents associate with free-market capitalism. It is part of the whole identity. Economic self-interest and individualism are not just "rational" or "efficient," they are what "real Americans" and "good Christians" value.

What do the bad people value? In her 2020 book *Socialists Don't Sleep: Christians Must Rise or America Will Fall*, conservative opinion

writer Cheryl Chumley explains, "Here's the real enemy: collec-
tivism." She goes on to say, "Far too many wolves run the church cir-
cuit these days, corrupting true biblical principles, undermining the
actual Word of God, creating a chaotic message that advances a dangerous far-left ideology in a country where far-left ideologies have
no right to exist. *Jesus wasn't a socialist*" (italics hers).[17] Think about
the juxtaposition of terms there: "true biblical principles" and "the
actual Word of God" versus a "dangerous far-left ideology" called
socialism. To follow Jesus and love America is to love individualism
and libertarian freedom, expressed in allegiance to capitalism and
unequivocal rejection of socialism.

In his speech at the "Evangelicals for Trump" rally on January 3,
2020, Donald Trump warned his audience:

> Our opponents want to shut out God from the public square so
> they can impose their extreme anti-religious and socialist agenda
> on America . . . The extreme left in America is trying to replace
> religion with government and replace God with socialism. That's
> what's happening . . . We resolve again today that America will
> never be a socialist country, ever. America was not built by
> religion-hating socialists. America was built by church-going,
> God-worshipping, freedom-loving patriots.

Similarly, in his 2020 book *United States of Socialism*, conservative
provocateur Dinesh D'Souza explains that socialists "would still
seek to demonize white males and push Christian symbols out of
the public square." D'Souza himself is not white and has no personal
experience being targeted as a white Christian man. But it's no co-
incidence that he references white men and Christians together.
In his mind, and likely that of his readers, the socialist assault on
one might as well be an assault on the other. And he exhorts his

readers in conclusion, "[W]e need a new generation of leaders who can assimilate the things that Trump does so effectively, fearlessly and gleefully. Trump has made it fun to beat the hell out of leftists and socialists, and even when Trump is gone, we must continue to enjoy the Trumpian experience of being a butt-kicking Republican, Christian, right-wing American capitalist."[18]

The dog whistle character of "Christian" language is on full display here. We might all be inclined to ask, "What exactly is 'Christian' about the 'Trumpian experience' D'Souza describes?" But inserting "Christian" in with that list of identities makes perfect sense if D'Souza is appealing to what political scientist Lilliana Mason calls a "mega-identity" that merges the various individual identities that distinguish "people like us" from "people like them."[19] And in both Trump's and D'Souza's statements, being a faithful American is connected to *both* promoting Christianity in the public square and opposition to those who would replace "our" culture and prosperous free markets with totalitarian socialism. D'Souza fuses the ethnic and economic threats together in a phrase he uses frequently: "identity socialism." Black Lives Matter? Democratic Socialists? Different names for the same enemy working to destroy "our" liberties.

In February 2021, we asked Americans how much they agreed that certain groups—conservative Christians, atheists, Muslims, and socialists—hold values that are morally inferior to those of people like them, want to limit the personal freedoms of people like them, and endanger the physical safety of people like them. We then added these up to make a scale measuring antipathy and fear toward each group. Unsurprisingly, white Americans who scored higher on white Christian nationalism thought conservative Christians were just fine, and they were more likely to hold prejudicial attitudes toward atheists, Muslims, and socialists. But here's what surprised us: the strongest association wasn't between white

Christian nationalism and antipathy or distrust toward atheists or Muslims. You might think that these groups pose the biggest threat to Americans who want a "*Christian* nation." Instead, the strongest connection was between white Christian nationalism and antipathy toward socialists. It is *that* group, not atheists or Muslims, that white Christian nationalism finds the most threatening.

Given this connection, it was unsurprising that when we ran regression models to assess which factors predicted higher scores on our anti-socialism scale, Christian nationalism was the biggest factor by a mile, even above conservative political ideology or partisan identification. It's what we call a "monster" in the model. This would immediately suggest that "socialists" appear to be most threatening, not necessarily for Republicans or those who are politically conservative per se, but principally for Americans who have merged the idea of Christian national identity with free-market capitalism.

But there's more. As we can see in Figure 1.10, the pattern exists among white Americans but not among Blacks. Black Americans' negative views toward socialists do not increase steadily no matter how high they score on our Christian nationalism scale. But white Americans nearly span the entire measure of antipathy and fear toward socialists as they increase in their adherence to Christian nationalism.

Thus it is not Americans in general who equate the idea of a Christian nation with free-market capitalism, but *white* Americans specifically.

We've explained that the term "Christian," because it has taken on an ethnic connotation in the minds of many whites, has become an invaluable dog whistle on the right to rally white conservatives to the defense of "our way of life," "our heritage," or

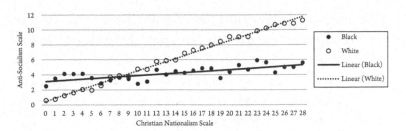

Figure 1.10. Predicted antipathy and fear toward socialists across Christian nationalism and race.

*Note:* Ordinary least squares regression models including Christian nationalism scale, political party identification, political conservatism, religious tradition, religiosity, age, gender, race, educational attainment, income, and region of the country. Significant interaction term between Christian nationalism × Black (p < .001).

*Source:* *Public Discourse and Ethics Survey (Wave 7; February 2021)*

"our country." But as Trump's rhetoric and that of his Christian right surrogates has shown, the word "socialist" has also become a critical dog whistle for white Americans who adhere to Christian nationalist ideology, helping to identify the "them" who pose such a grave threat to "us."

## CONCLUSION

It bears repeating once more that our Christian nationalism measures say absolutely nothing about race or the economy. And yet, for white Americans, a desire to institutionalize Christian identity and values in the public square is strongly related to a host of other ideas.

White Christian nationalism is our term for the ethno-traditionalism among many white Americans that conflates racial, religious, and national identity (the deep story) and pines for cultural and political power that demographic and cultural shifts have increasingly threatened (the vision). Though there have always been a variety of Christian groups and expressions, and we aren't simply "letting Christianity off the hook" here, the term "Christian" in white Christian nationalism is often far more akin to a dog whistle that calls out to an aggrieved tribe than a description of the content of one's faith. In Dinesh D'Souza's words, these days it means something like "butt-kicking Republican, Christian, right-wing American capitalist." Whiteness is often assumed in there.

As we've shown, the subtext of whiteness in the language of "Christian nation" and "Christian values" becomes obvious when we see how differently our Christian nationalism measures work for whites than for Black Americans. For Black Americans, adherence to Christian nationalism has little if any correlation with their views about racial discrimination, American religious history, COVID-19 issues, or views on the economy. And though we didn't show it here, it also has little bearing on Blacks' attitudes toward racial inequality, immigration, Islamophobia, or gun control once we account for other relevant characteristics.

But for white Americans, adherence to Christian nationalism is among the strongest predictors of ultraconservative stances on every contentious political issue. The ethno-traditionalism of white Christian nationalism then fosters white populism. We can see this when we consider which Americans were more likely to blame immigrants, the Chinese, or Blacks for the COVID-19 pandemic; which Americans trusted Donald Trump and Breitbart rather than experts and mainstream news for COVID-19 information; and which Americans prioritized personal liberty and economic prosperity over protecting vulnerable lives.

That connection between white Christian nationalism, personal liberty, and economic prosperity does much to shape our contemporary political landscape. How did these connections between whiteness, Christianity, and allegiance to libertarian free-market ideals first emerge and develop? The history goes back a lot further than you think.

# Chapter 2

# The Spirit of 1690

In 2019, the *New York Times* launched "the 1619 Project." Why "1619"? That year, 20 kidnapped Africans arrived off the coast of Port Comfort, in the English colony of Virginia. They were then sold into a lifetime of bondage. And so began the history of Black slavery in what would become the United States. In a series of podcasts, the leader of the project, journalist Nikole Hannah-Jones, traced the consequences of this moment up through the present day. Her claim that 1619 was as definitive a year as 1776 for the history of the country met with a mix of applause and outrage that broke along predictable party lines.[1]

In October 2020, shortly before losing his bid for re-election, then President Trump assembled a "1776 Commission" that included no professional historians, but was led by executives at the conservative Hilsdale College as well as Charlie Kirk and other intellectuals, politicians, and pundits. The Commission issued its hastily written report on January 18, 2021, less than two weeks after the Capitol Insurrection and only two days before Joe Biden took office. The authors insisted that "the United States has a definite birthday": not an unknown day in 1619, but "July 4, 1776." The report listed "slavery" as a "challenge to America's principles," alongside "fascism" and "communism" and also "progressivism" and "identity politics." Its claims met with a similarly mixed reception, also along predictable party lines.[2]

Between these two dates falls another crucial milestone—not a founding, exactly, but an inflection point. For it was around 1690 that racism, apocalypticism, and nationalism first fused into a deep story. It's important to emphasize that things could have turned out differently had some of the colonists acted differently. You could say that in 1690 we lost an alternative vision for life in the New World: one in which the natives and the colonists would live in concord or even in community; one in which the line between white and Black did not yet fully and irrevocably correspond to that between freedom and bondage; and one in which there was room, not only for non-Protestants but also for non-Christians. The death of that vision went hand in hand with the birth of a new vision: a social order dominated by white Protestant men and defined in opposition to "red savagery," Black bondage, and Roman popery. Within that order, race, religion, and nationalism were to be aligned—by force, if necessary. That is the spirit of 1690: the spirit of white Christian nationalism.

The original alignment of race, religion, and nation was repeatedly rejiggered in the centuries that followed, though never radically transformed. The bounds of whiteness were expanded to make room for successive waves of European immigrants. Only for Protestants at first, but eventually for Catholics and (some) Jews, who, it should be emphasized, were *not* considered white at first.[3] The borders of the nation expanded steadily westward to the Pacific and then beyond. The nation became an empire in which whites ruled and "races" multiplied: to "black" and "red" were added "brown" and "yellow." But while the cast of the deep story changed a great deal, the script itself changed very little. In the Spirit of 1690, whiteness connotes "freedom" and "order," but also "violence": freedom in opposition to Black bondage; order against native "savagery," and violence as the means of ensuring both.

Our vision is much closer to that of the 1619 Project than the 1776 Commission. But it also differs from both in important ways. Where the 1619 Project sees mostly continuity, we see much contingency. In 1619, a more inclusive and egalitarian society was still possible, if not probable. It was the decisions and actions of Puritan thinkers and leaders that throttled it. What's more, that possibility was choked off not only by the enslavement of kidnapped Africans, but also by warfare with native peoples—and their French Catholic allies. "Whiteness" was defined not only in opposition to "blackness" but also to "redness," and not only in terms of color but also in terms of religion: Protestant vs. Catholic and Christian vs. "heathen."[4] The first colonists committed two "original sins," not one. If we too often forget the first one—the violent expropriation of the indigenous peoples—it is partly because violence and disease left behind far fewer of their descendants to remind us. The Spirit of 1690 was to impose white control over non-white bodies, indigenous lands, and all political institutions.

As for the 1776 Commission, where it saw rupture, we see repetition. In 1776, a more inclusive and egalitarian society once again appeared possible, if only briefly. Some whites—and many non-whites—took the founding ideals of liberty and equality to their obvious and logical conclusion: abolition.[5] But the price of manumission was deemed too high, and national unity was bought at the expense of racial equality. That same pattern would repeat itself for a third time with the end of Reconstruction and a fourth time after the civil rights movement. Four times the dream of racial equality was sacrificed on the altar of (white) national unity. The question is whether history will repeat itself a fifth time in our own era. This much should be clear by now: realizing the dream of a multiracial democracy means abandoning the spirit of 1690 and the story—the "deep story"—that has sustained it for over three centuries. Instead we must find a new story—a better story—about what America can and should be. In what follows, we will also single out some white Christians who tried to write such a story.

Before we begin, a brief note on "periodization." Historians usually break up their narratives into successive eras or "periods." One way of periodizing American history is around "founding" events (Puritans and Revolution) and "refounding" moments (Civil War and Civil Rights). Another is around "great wars" (Revolution, Civil War, World War II). But the development of the deep story does not quite follow these rhythms. Its development was more often driven by America's oft-forgotten little wars (e.g., King Philipp's, French and Indian, Mexican-American, Spanish-American, and Cold War) and by population shifts (westward expansion, mass immigration) and changing religious demographics (Catholic, Jewish, and non-Christian immigration). In what follows, we focus on a different series of crucial moments, roughly speaking: 1689, 1763, 1889, and 1989. It was around 1690, following King Philipp's War, that the deep story first crystallized in the form of white Protestant chosenness. By the close of the French and Indian Wars in 1763, it had taken the form of Anglo Protestantism. By the end of the Spanish-American War in 1898, it had become WASP Imperialism. A century later, at the close of the Cold War, it had evolved into White Judaeo-Christian Americanism. How this evolution occurred and what these labels mean is the subject to which we now turn.


## SAINTS AND DEMONS, PURITANS AND "INDIANS"

Who were the Puritans? It is a tricky question, a bit like defining "evangelical" today. The term encompassed a wide range of theological positions and various forms of religious community. Writing in 1581, the English Puritan Perceval Wilburn cheekily described his religious compatriots as "the hotter sort of Protestants": those who burned with religious zeal—and were also sometimes *literally* burned for it. Many historians have made this definition their own. More recently, journalist James Sleeper has ambivalently described the Puritan refugees who fled to a New England as "America's first Very Serious People," people who were serious about their moral principles.[6] And also serious about enforcing them (including on non-Puritans).

If there was one thing the Puritans took very seriously though, it was their Bible. They didn't just read the Bible. In a way, they read themselves *into* the Bible. For the Puritans understood them-selves as—literally—a "New Israel," and they slowly came to see New England as their "Promised Land." Not all at once or from the outset. The first Puritan settlers still saw New England as a "howling wilderness." England was their real home, their Promised Land, and they expected to return there one day. Like the God-fearing Israelites whom the Babylonians had cast out of Jerusalem, so, too, would they one day return to their homeland and their capital city and be restored to honor and glory. But that day would never come. Puritans—and Catholics—did rule premodern England, but only briefly. England would ultimately remain in the hands of the cooler sort of Protestants, the very sorts the Puritans desperately sought to escape. If the Puritans were to have a Promised Land, it would have to be New England.[7]

Few played a more prominent role in crafting this vision of New England as a New Israel than the Mathers, Cotton (1663–1728) and his father and grandfather, Increase and Richard Mather. Today, Cotton is most often remembered for his role in the Salem witch trials of 1692. But he was also one of the first chroniclers of New England—and of its wars with the natives. For the secular reader,

Mather's chronicle seems a curious hodgepodge of military and church history. There are long descriptions of battles between the New England colonists and various native tribes, but also entire chapters on Baptist and Quaker dissenters. For Mather, though, war and dissent were inextricably linked by covenant and providence. In his view, the Puritans had made a covenant with God to defend the true religion. The presence of dissenters was a breach of this covenant. God punished the Puritans for that breach by sending the natives to wage war on them. In Mather's words, "since this degeneracy has obtained so much among us, the wrath of heaven has raised up against us a succession of other adversaries and calamities." If heretics were the cause of God's wrath, then the natives were his chosen instrument. As with the biblical Israelites of the Old Testament, so with his new Chosen People in their new Promised Land of New England.[8]

Mather was not the first to view the Puritans' wars with the native tribes through a providential lens. But he was arguably the first to view it through an apocalyptic lens as well. Viewed through the first lens, the Puritans' wars with the natives were a—literal—repeat of the Israelites' wars with the Canaanites; viewed through the second lens, they were also part of the apocalyptic battle between the forces of Christ and the Anti-Christ. Either way, the message was the same: the Puritans' wars were holy wars, the native lands were to be Puritan lands, and the expulsion and extermination of the natives was a righteous sacrifice to an angry God.[9]

It must be stressed that Mather's was not the only vision. Where he preached elimination, other Puritans pursued conversion, though by that they meant conversion not just to a creed or a church but to an entire way of life. On this view, the dominant view, to be a Christian was to live like an English person (i.e., to settle in one place, to work the land, to own personal property, to practice monogamy, to wear trousers, and to accept one's providential station in life). To this end, Puritan missionaries such as John Eliot established several dozen settlements of "praying Indians" in Massachusetts. Like Mather, Eliot saw the native tribes through biblical lenses. But his lenses were ground a little differently than Mather's. Eliot saw the native tribes as the lost tribes of Israel. And he hoped that by gathering them together, he was helping to bring about Christ's return. But Eliot's dream was shattered by the brutal conflict generally known as "King Philipp's War." So were many of the praying villages he helped establish. That war, in which 30 to 40% of the English population was killed, and native tribes suffered even more devastating losses, challenged the Puritans' understanding of themselves and their understanding of the "New World."[10]

It's important to stress that killing or converting Indians were not the only possibilities entertained by the Puritans. There was also a third: coexistence. The first to theorize and practice it was Roger Williams (1603–1683). Though a Puritan, Williams quickly fell out with his brethren and was banished from Boston. He then established the Providence Colony in what is now Rhode Island. Williams developed close ties with the native tribes. He sometimes preached the gospel to his native acquaintances. But he did not attempt to change their way of life. For him, being a Christian did not require living like an Englishman. Under Williams' leadership, the Providence Colony became a haven for dissent and a beacon of toleration—and also an early prototype of what a multiracial and multicultural democracy might look like.

It's important to understand why. It was not because Williams himself was "ecumenical" or "respectful." He was not. But Williams's views differed from Mather's in at least three key respects. First, he drew a sharp line between Christianity and morality: the one did not imply the other. In his observation, the morality of the natives was often superior to that of the Puritans. Second, he drew a sharp line between religious and civil authority, much sharper even than the Puritans, not because he worried about the church corrupting the state but rather the reverse. Third, because he believed that freedom of conscience was absolute, and that it implied freedom of expression. He rejected the collective authority of the Puritan clergy and, even more, their efforts to silence dissent. In sum, Williams believed that people of the most varied backgrounds could still form a civil society together, so long as they separated religion and morality and church and state and did not force anyone's conscience or silence anyone's speech. This he called "meer civility."[11] Sadly, the path of "meer civility" was the road less traveled in Williams's day. Killing and converting would become the dominant poles of "Indian policy" in the centuries that followed.

The deep story was coming together. But it was not yet complete. Mather had woven together the Promised Land and the End Times in his narrative of New England's history up through King Philipp's War. His version of white Christian nationalism might be called "white Puritan chosen-ness." But the racist strand of the deep story was still underdeveloped in his writing. One does find proto-racist ideas in Mather. He often described the natives in dehumanizing and demonizing language, as animals or devil-worshipers. Further, he sometimes claimed that divine salvation was a matter of biological descent; chosen-ness ("election") was passed down from parents to children via "loins" and flowed in the "blood." But a thicker, tauter version of the racist thread was being spun together further south, in the colony of Virginia. Its original purpose was to bind the Black "bondsmen" and make their enslavement heritable. All too often, the master weavers were Christian clergy.

## SLAVE AND FREE IN BLACK AND WHITE

In the premodern era, most Christian theologians agreed that there were two types of people who could be justifiably enslaved: "heathens" and "captives" of war. "Indians" and "Negroes" were not the only persons in the southern colonies who fit these categories. Irish Catholics did too. England's colonization of North America and its conquest of Ireland overlapped in time and influenced each other. For example, English commentators often described the Catholic Irish as "heathens" and sometimes even as "Indians" in order to justify the seizure of Irish property and establishment of English "plantations" on the "Emerald Isle." Nor was the legal status of Irish-Catholic indentured servants in the American colonies altogether different from that of enslaved Blacks and Natives, at least not at first. That would change. For a new racial order was emerging in the New World, an order in which "white" meant "free," "black" meant "slave," and "red" meant neither bound nor free but "savage."[12]

The reasons for this shift from various forms of nonracial bondage to a system of Black slavery were largely economic: the turn to labor-intensive cash crops such as tobacco and sugar; the shortage of white labor in the colonies; the constant flight of enslaved natives who knew the land better than their captors; and, finally, the flood of kidnapped Africans onto the Atlantic slave market that followed the foundation of the British Royal Africa Company and the Dutch West India Company.[13]

But the shift to Black slavery created a problem for English theologians, a problem that grew more acute as some enslaved Blacks converted to Christianity and enslavement was passed on from mother to child. On what grounds could Christians enslave other Christians—Christians, moreover, who were not captives of war? The old theological justifications provided no clear answer. New justifications had to be invented. What was needed, in a phrase, was a racist theology.

The need was soon met. Writing in 1681, the Anglican priest Morgan Godwyn listed the two most common forms of racist theology. The first was "pre-Adamism," the belief that there had been two separate creations resulting in two separate species: pre-Adamites and Adamites. Only the latter were humans with souls. The second was Noah's Curse: because Ham had seen Noah drunk and naked in his tent, God placed a mark on Ham's son Canaan and condemned his offspring to perpetual servitude.[14]

By 1700, proslavery theologians had woven these and other stories together into what historian David Whitford calls the "Curse Matrix." It had three elements: (1) "black skin is the result of God's curse"; (2) so is Africans' supposed "hypersexuality and libidinousness"; and (3) slavery was actually a boon to Africans because it exposed them to Christianity and (white) civilization.[15]

Of course, if theology delivered some of the most influential arguments for Black enslavement, it also provided some of the most powerful counterarguments against it. Take one contemporary of Godwyn's, Judge Samuel Sewall. In 1700, Sewall published "The Selling of Joseph," generally regarded as the first antislavery tract written in the English colonies. In it, Sewall sought to refute several common theological justifications of slavery. He argued that "all Men are Sons of Adam, are Co-heirs, and have equal right unto Liberty." And he argued that the Curse of Ham did not apply to Africans. The first argument was the more consequential: all humans are of one blood and therefore entitled to equal rights.[16] It was an argument that would be echoed by later generations of Christian abolitionists and by civil rights activists up through the present day, when they insist that all human beings are made in the "image of God."

In colonial Virginia though, the Curse of Ham won out over the Image of God. As so often happens, the theology followed the money. Like Williams's, Sewall's was the path less traveled. But it marked out the road that Christian abolitionists and civil rights activists would follow in the future.

By 1700, then, the three narrative threads that comprise white Christian nationalism's deep story had each been spun together in the British colonies, two in the North, and one in the South. But they were only loosely nationalistic and not at all "American." What fused them together into a single thread? And what made that thread "American"? Put simply, what transformed white Puritan chosenness into white Protestant Americanism? The answer once again is the heat of war, or, rather a series of wars. Not wars with the natives, though, so much as wars with and between France and England.

## EMPIRE AND WAR IN THE MAKING OF WHITE PROTESTANT AMERICA

Americans are accustomed to thinking of the Revolution as a battle for freedom from England. But this frame is too narrow. If we widen our view a bit, the Revolution appears in a very different light, as part of much wider and longer struggle between the rulers and nations of Europe for control over the land and riches of "the New World." The theater of war encompassed most of North America and Western Europe. The leading roles in the conflict are taken by the colonial powers of Europe—England, of course, but also France, Spain, and the Netherlands. Their North American colonists really only play bit parts in the contest until quite late in the game. The various native tribes were often more important—and arguably more powerful—than the colonists.[17] This centuries-long drama opens with the arrival of the Spanish in the 15th century and closes when Mexico and then Canada gain their independence during the mid-19th century.[18]

Now let's zoom back in a bit on the key context for our story—the story of white Christian nationalism in what becomes the United States. The key actors in this part of the action are England and France and their colonies, the native tribes that inhabited the Eastern Seaboard and the Great Lakes region, and enslaved Africans living in the Southeast. The key events are two wars or rather series of wars: (1) the French and Indian Wars (1688–1763) and (2) the American Revolution (1775–1783) and the War of 1812.[19] The stakes are land and resources, power and money. But what interests us here is not so much the outcome of the struggle—fateful as that was, especially for the native peoples—as its effects on the colonists and their culture.

The two sets of wars affected the English colonies very differently. The first phase brought them much closer to the "Motherland." At perhaps no other time did the colonists feel themselves more "British" than during their struggle against the Catholic French and their native allies during the French and Indian Wars (1688–1763). The second phase pushed them far apart. At perhaps no other time did England's (former) colonists feel less "British" than after the Revolution and during the War of 1812. In sum, white Christian nationalism became "British" in phase one and then "American" in phase two.[20] It was the heat of war that really fused religion, race, and nation together into white Christian nationalism.

It was also during this period, that the holy trinity of white Christian nationalism—that peculiar nexus of freedom, order, and violence—really first crystallized.[21] To be "British" during the 18th century was also to be "Protestant" and "free," and therefore to be anti-French.[22] For Protestants were not free in France; they were a persecuted minority. And English Catholics were (supposedly) against freedom; they were viewed as a dangerous minority bent on tyranny. So, to be free was to be Protestant and British.[23]

But the "freedom" of Protestant Englishmen was only possible if the racial order was maintained; and that often required the exercise of violence against racial others. On the frontier, that meant natives who controlled land and other resources, such as furs. In the colonies, that meant enslaved Blacks, who were both a source and a form of wealth to white slavers. The threat to "white freedom" appeared all the greater, insofar as both groups were sometime allies of England's imperial rivals.[24] These threats to the racial order—and to private wealth—had to be met with brutal violence; and they were.

The French and Indian Wars were like a crucible in which whiteness was forged. What began as a fight among European powers for control of land and resources was transformed as colonists of English descent allied with others of European descent to defend "white" rule. Out of this crucible came a new racial hierarchy, painted in white, red, and Black: white on top, Black on the bottom, and red in between.[25]

The French and Indian Wars generated a British and Protestant version of white Christian nationalism in the colonies; the Revolutionary War and the War of 1812 helped to "Americanize" it. Until the Revolution, most colonists identified as "British" or "English"; the term "American" usually referred to the native peoples. After the Revolution, the former colonists struggled to articulate what was "American" about the United States. They often answered that question by appropriating native culture. What supposedly made white American men different from their former British countrymen was that they also had a tinge of "red" and a bit of the "savage" in them. The first symbol of this white American masculinity was not the "cowboy" but the "scout," the frontiersman who ventured into the wild, learned the ways of the "Indian," and absorbed a bit of "savagery" in the process.[26] The figure of the scout, in other words, was the first heroic embodiment of the individualistic ethos that is at the heart of white Christian nationalism and its holy trinity of freedom, order, and violence.

In the Southern states, this association between white freedom and male violence was stronger still. For there, freedom and violence were linked, not only by the threat of native war bands on a distant frontier, but also by fears of Black insurrection on local plantations. This is one reason why so many of the revolutionaries defined "freedom," not only in opposition to "tyranny," but to "slavery" as well.[27] To be sure, they understood "slavery" broadly; it referred to any form of dependency or subservience to the will of another. Chattel slavery was just its most extreme form. But for some, especially in the Southern colonies, Black slavery was also the bedrock foundation of a certain kind of white freedom. Relieved of the burdens of physical labor, rich Southern planters such as Washington and Jefferson were free to dabble in science and engage in politics. Even in times of peace, preserving their personal liberty meant depriving others of theirs, by violent means when necessary.

White fear was even greater during times of war, when some enslaved Blacks sided with America's enemies in the hope of winning their own freedom. Much has been made of the small number of free Blacks who joined the "patriot cause" during the Revolution. But there were many more enslaved Blacks who fled their American enslavers and joined the British forces in hopes of securing their freedom.[28]

This was also true in the War of 1812. Indeed, the British marine units that stormed the US Capitol included many Blacks soldiers who had fled slavery. Seen in this context, the third stanza of the

Star Spangled Banner (composed in 1814) appears in a much more sinister light.

> Their blood has wash'd out their foul footstep's pollution.
> No refuge could save the hireling and slave
> From the terror of flight or the gloom of the grave,
> And the star-spangled banner in triumph doth wave
> O'er the land of the free and the home of the brave.

In other words, the blood of Black British soldiers slain by white American "heroes" washed away the "pollution" left by their Black bodies on the sacred grounds of the Capitol. White freedom was bought with Black blood. The holy trinity of white Christian nationalism is written right into the national anthem of the United States.

It goes without saying that most Black Americans saw through this mythology. But so did some white Christians. For some revolutionaries, whiteness, Protestantism, American-ness, freedom, and violence defined "the Spirit of 1776." But not for all. For early Quaker abolitionists, such as Anthony Benezet and Warner Mifflin, Black enslavement was not only a "National Sin" but a violation of the Golden Rule—the most basic tenet of Christian morality. There could be no such thing as "Christian Slavery" nor a "Christian slaveholder"; both were contradictions in terms.

Of course, Christians weren't alone in this. For some Enlightenment rationalists such as Benjamin Franklin and Thomas Paine, the institution of slavery violated the ideals of equality and freedom for which the Revolution had been waged. For still others, such as the Christian physician and social reformer Benjamin Rush, there was no contradiction between Christianity and democracy; each reinforced the other—and each opposed slavery. What all these men had in common, besides their hatred of slavery, was their roots in Pennsylvania. What Roger Williams's Providence Colony had been to the 17th century, William Penn's Colony was to the 18th: an early experiment in multiracial, multireligious democracy. That popular histories of the Revolution focus so much attention on New England and Virginia is a form of collective amnesia about what might have been, of the elusive possibility of a multiracial republic that appeared (again and for a second time) during and after the Revolution.[29]

Political realists might respond that this experiment was doomed to failure from the start, and that the price of the Constitution was the perpetuation of slavery. Historian Gary Nash disputes this conclusion. That this did not happen, he concludes, was due, not just to the intransigence of Southern slave owners, but to the cowardice of Northern politicians—and the avarice of Northern slave traders. In Nash's reckoning, the Founders' compromise on slavery was not just immoral; it was unnecessary and self-interested.[30]

By the end of the War of 1812, white Christian nationalism had become both Protestant and American. And it had developed a particular understanding of freedom, order, and violence—grounded in a specific kind of individualism. As the United States expanded outward and then westward, white Christian nationalism would be distilled still further, into what we call "WASP imperialism." Once again, the crucial catalyst was war, not for North America, this time, but for Cuba.


## THE CLOSING OF THE FRONTIER AND THE MAKING OF WHITE CHRISTIAN EMPIRE

If the 1690s were a formative decade for white Christian nationalism—and its holy trinity of freedom, order, and violence—then the 1890s were a transformative one. There were two catalysts for this transformation: the closing of the American frontier and the beginning of the American Empire. The result of the transformation was threefold: changed understandings of whiteness, divine providence, and national identity. The spirit of 1690 was reborn as WASP Imperialism.

The spirit of 1690 adapted easily enough to life on the 19th-century frontier. It encountered many familiar faces there: the "red" faces of the native tribes that were being driven steadily and violently westward and corralled into so-called reservations by century's end and the Black faces of enslaved persons who were involuntarily marched or transported westward and onto new plantations from Kentucky to Texas. That white men used violence to "protect" their freedom (and to seize others' property) was nothing new.

The spirit of 1690 also encountered new faces on the frontier: the "brown" faces of Mexican citizens who suddenly found themselves on American territory as Texas, California, and large swaths of the Southwest were forcibly incorporated into the United States following the Mexican-American War (1846–1848); and also the "yellow" faces of Chinese and Japanese immigrants to the Pacific coast beginning with the California gold rush of 1848. Here, too, irregular militias and vigilante justice were critical means of moving the frontier westward and establishing white freedom. Then, as before, racial conflict and white Christian nationalism evolved in tandem with violent white men starring as the hero-protagonists who enforced the racial order.[31]

To the spirit of 1690 the new faces looked an awful lot like the old ones. Dehumanizing racial and religious stereotypes first developed to justify war against the natives and the enslavement of Africans were quickly adapted to new "others." Asian immigrants were derided as an inferior race of "heathens" unfit for citizenship in a "Christian republic." Asian women were seen as hypersexualized temptresses, unsuited for marriage or motherhood. Mexicans were classified as a "mongrel race" whose Catholic faith had inured them to despotism. There was perhaps some hope for Mexican women but only if they were paired with white Protestant men. Brown and yellow actors could be cast in roles once reserved for red and Black actors with only minor adjustments to the script.[32]

But other developments in this era would eventually force a major rewrite of the deep story. The first was the Civil War. In the Reconstruction era (1865–1877), when Union troops occupied the defeated Confederacy, emancipated Blacks could vote freely, and abolitionist Republicans controlled Congress, a truly radical rewrite of the American story again seemed possible, a re-envisioning of the United States as a multiracial democracy. But that vision was rejected by Northern Democrats and then buried by rehabilitated Confederates. These self-styled Southern "Redeemers" developed a whitewashed account of the Civil War, the myth of the "Lost Cause." In this narrative, the Civil War became a "War of Northern Aggression" in which soldiers of the Confederacy fought to defend "states' rights," and Reconstruction was a period of "Negro misrule" abetted by greedy "carpetbaggers" from the North. It was white Southern women—Daughters of the Confederacy—who seared the Lost Cause myth into the collective memory of the Old Confederacy. They did so through public rituals, such as Memorial Day; public monuments to Confederate heroes; and, last but not least, by teaching the Lost Cause myth to generations of Southern children.[33]

The Lost Cause myth introduced a new scriptural wrinkle into white Christian nationalism. It foretold that the Old South would "rise again" one day, like the crucified Christ, its suffering transfigured into glory. This, too, was a form of white Christian nationalism derived from Christian scripture, but one based on themes of crucifixion and redemption rather than Promised Lands or End Times. It is crucial to understanding contemporary claims of Christian victimhood and vengeance among white Christian nationalists.[34]

The second key development was theological. After the Revolution, Northern Protestant theologians began subtly redefining the End Times story. For Cotton Mather, recall, the Second Coming of Christ and his thousand-year reign on Earth would be preceded by a cosmic war between good and evil—the Battle of Armageddon. Because the End Times *preceded* Christ's millennial return, the technical term for Mather's interpretation is "premillennial apocalypticism." But the dominant view of the white Protestant establishment during the 19th century was actually "postmillennial": Christ would return only *after* the Kingdom of God had been established on Earth for a full thousand years by means of gradual social and moral reform led by the Christian churches. Northern theologians such as Horace Greeley (1811–1872) and Josiah Strong (1847–1916) then combined this new postmillennial view of the End Times with the old Promised Land story. The result was the doctrine of "Manifest Destiny." White Americans were still a chosen people. But their task was not just to build a "city on a hill" in New England but to "civilize" an entire continent. Their westward movement was part of a divine plan. The great pre-Revolutionary revivalist and theologian, Jonathan Edwards (1703–1758) had already noted that Christ's gospel had always moved from East to West—from the Middle East to Western Europe on to North America. That it should continue its triumphant march all the way to the shores of the Pacific was nothing short of providential.[35]

The third development was "racial": a changed understanding of whiteness that was more "scientific" and also more "shaded." In the aftermath of the French and Indian Wars, the Bible was the main basis on which the various "races" were classified and racial inequality explained; "white" was a catch-call category opposed to "black" and then "red." By the late 19th century, accounts of race often appealed to "science" as well.[36] Some "race scientists" claimed that the various races had evolved separately; others argued that racial differences expressed themselves in physical characteristics that could be precisely measured; still others placed more emphasis on cultural differences. So-called germ theorists made vague, scientific-sounding claims about the racial, physical, and cultural superiority of "Aryans," "Nordics," or "White Anglo-Saxon Protestants" who were the supposed bearers of an invisible "germ" of civilization, a people destined to conquer and rule the world. On this account, widely embraced by America's Protestant establishment, whites were still superior to non-whites, but now some whites were whiter than others. Meanwhile, in the South, a new term was invented for whites who commingled and intermarried with non-whites: "white trash." This new, hierarchical theory of whiteness was especially attractive to native-born and middle-class white Americans during the second half of the 19th century because it explained why they were superior to the newly arriving Catholic and Jewish immigrants from Southern and Eastern Europe—and also why they and their fellow Anglo-Saxons were meant to conquer the world.[37]

Which brings us back, at last, to the topic of empire. The word was not really foreign to the vocabulary of 19th-century Americans. Thomas Jefferson had famously envisioned an "empire of liberty" comprising the United States and Canada, for example.[38] Nor was the law of empire foreign to the Constitution Jefferson had helped author. It distinguished between sovereign "states" where constitutional rights applied and subject "territories" where they did not, such as the Northwest Territory established in 1795 and the first

Indian Territory established in 1803. In principle, the residents of a territory could petition for statehood upon meeting certain requirements. In practice, the approval of such requests hinged on the religious and racial composition of the population. In 1849, for example, the Mormon leader Brigham Young proposed to establish a vast western state named "Deseret." At that time, Mormons were widely regarded as heretics, and Congress summarily rejected the proposal. It likewise rejected the initial petitions for statehood from Arizona and New Mexico, essentially on the grounds that their populations were insufficiently white. As for the Indian Territory established by the Creek confederation, it was dissolved by Andrew Jackson, despite having all the trappings of republicanism and "civilization," including a written constitution, an elected president, and several indigenous-language newspapers. Only Anglo Protestants were "real Americans." Everyone else was a second-class citizen—at best.[39]

Ironically, the American Empire began as an attempt to end the Spanish Empire. A pattern was thereby set: America's crusades for democracy led to the extension of its empire. The Spanish-American War began in 1898 in much the same way that subsequent American wars would: as an armed intervention into a civil war with the stated aim of "liberating" an oppressed people from tyranny. In this case, the war was in Cuba. From there, it moved on to the Philippines, Guam, and Puerto Rico. It was the beginning of an empire.

It was war that had solidified the Spirit of 1690; and it was war that transformed it into the Spirit of 1898. Or, rather, it was the series of overseas wars that began that year—and that continues into the present day. The new Spirit differed from the Old in at least three important ways. First, taking a cue from the South's Lost Cause myth, the new Spirit portrayed America's imperial adventurism as a form of noble self-sacrifice. Like Christ—and the Protestant theologians of the era did not hesitate for a moment to draw that comparison—America was acting out of compassion, altruism, and benevolence, never vengefulness, self-interest, or greed. America's motives were always and ever innocent, perfectly so. Even when it employed the most savage violence, it was doing God's will. There was a secular justification, too, and this is the second change. When America employs violence, this argument goes, it does so to spread freedom to others. On the frontier and on the plantation, violence had been used to establish and secure white freedom. Now, military violence would be used to spread the blessings of freedom throughout the world. All of America's imperial wars were and are wars of liberation, by definition. Once again, we see how white Christian nationalism is entangled with the holy trinity of racial order, Christian freedom, and male violence.

The high mass of white Christian nationalism was celebrated only periodically. It, too, culminated in the ritual sacrifice of human blood, in this case, the blood of those charged with violating the racial order: non-whites thought to have transgressed the color line, often Black men accused of sexual improprieties toward white women.[40] Whether they were actually guilty of the charges leveled at them was immaterial. The point was to draw whites together and unite them through their moral complicity in grisly acts of extrajudicial murder. The ritualized violence at the lynching tree was, of course, just the most extreme form of the racialized rituals that reinforced the color line in the everyday life of the Jim Crow South. And not only there. Outside the South, Jewish, Chinese, and Mexican Americans were the victims of mob violence as well.[41]

But what, some might ask, did these gruesome rituals have to do with Christianity? A great deal. Christian clergy sometimes participated in lynchings or even gave them their blessings. And the racial terrorists of the KKK were not just anti-Black racists. They purported to defend the supremacy of white Protestants against Catholics and Jews as well. Of course, there were also politer, more genteel forms of white Christian nationalism, found behind the closed parlor doors of the so-called White Citizen's Councils. But they were no less racist for all their gentility.[42]

And who nurtured the new Spirit of 1898? Looking back from the present, one might suppose that it was conservative, evangelical Protestants. In fact, it was more often liberal, mainline Protestants, people who prided themselves on being open to new ideas, such as Darwinism or biblical criticism. Many of the sharpest critics of the new Spirit were theological conservatives who held fast to Creationism and literalism and resisted free-market capitalism and American militarism: people such as three-time Democratic presidential candidate William Jennings Bryan.[43] That would change, as conservative evangelicals took control over the deep story.

## THE SPIRIT OF 1989: (WHITE) JUDEO-CHRISTIAN NATION

For over two centuries, from 1689 to 1898, white Christian nationalism was championed by the "Protestant Establishment." By 1989 the torch had been passed on to conservative white evangelicals. Over the course of the previous century, many white liberal Protestants had become secular progressives—and also liberal Democrats. Meanwhile, most white evangelicals had become conservative Republicans, and also pro-market and pro-military.

Why the radical reversal?

Contemporary conservatives often make *Roe v. Wade* the turning point in the story. In this account, the Religious Right emerged out of opposition to abortion. But the facts don't really fit that story particularly well. Conservative white Protestants did not become pro-life until the late 1970s. Before that, Protestants were divided on the question and abortion was seen as a "Catholic" issue. The rightward turn of white evangelicals actually began a quarter-century earlier with another Supreme Court case: *Brown v. Board of Education*. The political architects of the Religious Right—Paul Weyrich and Richard Viguerie—were quite clear on this point. Opposition to racial integration was the real catalyst for the rise of the Religious Right. Race was the wedge that split off white evangelicals from the Democratic Party. "Family values" was just the political cement Republican strategists used to bind white evangelicals to their old arch-enemies: conservative Catholics.[44]

How did this influence white Christian nationalism?

Conservative white evangelicals made three important changes to the white Christian nationalist script. First, they reverted to the premillennialist version of the End Times story.[45] The horrors of the World Wars and the invention of atomic weapons had made the fiery battle scenes of Revelation seem more real than metaphorical. And predictions of nuclear holocaust were also promises of deliverance and vengeance: true believers could view the nuclear Armageddon secure in the knowledge that it heralded Jesus's return. It should be little surprise that by the middle 2000s, one of the strongest predictors that white Americans affirm Christian nationalist ideology is their confidence that literal Rapture and Armageddon events will take place, in which the faithful are caught up to be with Jesus followed by a war of God's faithful against "the Beast" of Revelation (see Figure 2.1).

Second, they gradually shifted from white supremacism to "color-blindness." At first, the shift was purely tactical. Instead of shouting the n-word, conservative white leaders now tut-tutted about "welfare queens."[46] The "Curse of Cain" was reborn as the

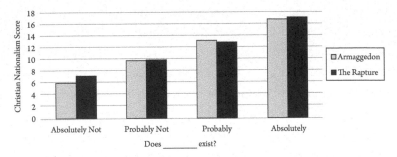

Figure 2.1. Predicted adherence to Christian nationalism across belief in a literal Rapture and Armageddon.

**Note:** Ordinary least squares regression models predicting Christian nationalism scale. Controls include political party identification, political conservatism, religious tradition, religiosity, beliefs about the Bible, age, gender, educational attainment, income, and region of the country.

**Source:** 2007 Baylor Religion Survey

"Culture of Poverty." Later, it became more "personal." "Racial reconciliation" was the watchword, as if Blacks needed to offer an apology for their own oppression. But the key was that race should not be "politicized." The only way to address racism, in this view, was to "change hearts," or better yet, to stop talking about race altogether. Changing laws was not necessary. Paying reparations was out of the question. Racism was a personal problem, not a social one.[47] Social justice was derided as "un-Christian." Conservative color-blindness was and remains today, in effect, a form of anti-anti-racism, a way of deflecting demands for racial justice.

The third and final shift was the focus on sexual sin. Of course, the focus on sex was not entirely new; it went back to the New England Puritans and beyond. After all, they invented the "scarlet letter!" What was new was the near exclusive focus on sex as the most dangerous form of sin. The Puritans had been equally concerned with other transgressions, such as drunkenness, covetousness, idleness, and immodest dress. The Methodists and Baptists of the 19th century also worried about "upright" living and personal "holiness." For conservative white evangelicals on the other hand, "Christian morality" was increasingly equated with sexual morality.[48]

The net result of these three shifts was a hyper-aggressive foreign policy, a laissez-faire economic policy, and attempts to legislate sexual morality.

The individualist component of white Christian nationalism was also changing in the decades after World War II, becoming color-blind "Christian libertarianism." Secular progressives are often puzzled by this pairing. It seems like a marriage of convenience. Or maybe just an oxymoron. After all, one says "thou shalt not," while the other says leave me alone. One says, "blessed are the poor," but the other says "greed is good." Aren't Christianity and capitalism fundamentally at odds? Not for the Christian libertarian.

## THE OTHER SPIRIT OF 1989: (WHITE) CHRISTIAN LIBERTARIANISM

In *One Nation Under God: How Corporate America Invented Christian America,* Princeton historian Kevin Kruse recounts the career of the California minister Kevin Fifield and his pro-business organization, Spiritual Mobilization.[49] Fifield hobnobbed with rich businessmen. He also lived like one, sporting tailored suits and driving fast cars. In many ways, he was the prototype of the prosperity gospel preacher of our own era—minus the designer sneakers. At the same time, Fifield happily supported President Eisenhower's efforts to conjure up a Christian—and capitalist—America to fight the "Godless communism" of the Soviet

Union. And he did so with the support of conservative Christian businessmen like J. Howard Pew.

Conservative white businessmen and theologians were not the only ones in the kitchen cooking up Christian libertarianism. Southern white racists also had a finger in the pot. For example, Strom Thurmond, the long-serving Senator from South Carolina, began his career as a progressive Democrat and ended it as a conservative Republican.[50] The civil rights movement was the key inflection point. For Thurmond, choosing between white supremacism and economic equality was not difficult. He intuited—correctly—that many other whites felt the same way, and not just in the South. Thurmond's "Southern Strategy" was not just a strategy for bringing the Old Confederacy into the Republican fold, however. It was also a means of exporting small-town Southern politics to Northern whites hostile to racial equality, and to white suburban Southerners too polite to use the "n-word."[51] The means to this end was the libertarian language of "free markets" and "private property" in tandem with racial dog-whistles like "welfare dependency" and "crime waves." For many white Americans, libertarian rhetoric was really just a polite, "color-blind" way of being racist.

Christian libertarianism did not really become a major force in American politics until the Reagan Era. Here, too, the crucial turning point was civil rights. Evangelical resistance to desegregation could no longer be couched in explicitly racist terms. Libertarianism provided a politer language. Consider the case of Jerry Falwell. He is best known as the cofounder of the "Moral Majority," an evangelical advocacy organization at the forefront of the "culture wars."[52] But he was also an aggressive champion of "free markets." Like Strom Thurmond, he embraced libertarian rhetoric as a means of rejecting demands for racial equality without resorting to racialized rhetoric. Falwell's evolution from segregationist to libertarian was a common one.

Insofar as there was a "systematic theology" that integrated Christian libertarianism and Christian nationalism, it was the work of the "Christian Reconstructionists" or "theonomists," a small but influential movement centered around Rousas John Rushdoony, an ultraconservative Presbyterian pastor who settled in Orange County.[53] He argued that the American government and society had to be "reconstructed" according to "Biblical law."

Rushdoony was also a Christian libertarian, in the general sense that he was strongly pro-capitalist and vehemently anti-communist. But it was really his son-in-law, Gary North, who attempted to synthesize neoclassical economics and Calvinist theology into some sort of coherent whole.[54] This was not as difficult as it may sound, at least within the particular tradition of Dutch Calvinism to which North and his father-in-law both adhered.[55] Like all good Calvinists, North took a rather dim view of human goodness that comported well with neoclassical assumptions about the inevitability of self-interested behavior. Because humans are inherently sinful, the best way to organize an economy is to channel their self-interest via the market. Free markets are also the best way to punish vice and reward virtue, to assure that everyone gets their just desserts. Government regulation is not only inefficient, on this view, it is also un-Christian. Following the Dutch Calvinist, Abraham Kuyper, North also believed that God had divided human life into various "spheres," which were independent of one another, but all of which were under divine sovereignty. This meant that the state must not "intervene" in the economy. As for federal taxation for purposes of economic redistribution, North regarded it as a form of "theft" that violated the Seventh Commandment. North eventually moved from

California to Texas, where he became a close adviser of libertarian congressman and Republican presidential candidate Ron Paul.

If Gary North was the greatest systematizer of Christian libertarianism, then Dave Ramsey is arguably its greatest popularizer.[56] Ramsey lives in a multimillion-dollar home outside Nashville and manages a staff of nearly 700 people at his gleaming headquarters nearby. He has a self-syndicated radio show that airs weekdays on over 300 radio stations across the country. He has preached his gospel at thousands of churches around the country. His immense wealth notwithstanding, Ramsey's gospel is not the prosperity gospel; it is an austerity gospel. In his 20s, Ramsey was a free-spending real estate mogul with a healthy appetite for high living. Until he went bankrupt, that is. For him, the conversion to austerity and Christianity went hand in hand. Not surprisingly, Ramsey's politics lean libertarian—Christian libertarian. Like North, he decries taxes as "theft" and derides "Social Insecurity."[57] It goes without saying that he is "pro-gun" and "pro-police." If North's is the egghead's version of Christian libertarianism, then Ramsey's is the mass-market one.

## CONCLUSION: BACK TO THE BULL HORN?

In some ways, white Christian nationalism has changed a great deal over the last three-plus centuries. The boundaries of whiteness expanded to include not just Englishmen but anyone of European descent. The meaning of "Christian" was loosened to include Catholics and Mormons and even hyphenated to include (some "good") Jews. Hubristic talk of American "chosen-ness" was toned down to the seemingly more modest claim of "American exceptionalism." Gory talk of "blood sacrifice" was watered down into the euphemistic rhetoric of "ultimate sacrifice." The racial and religious undertones were still there, of course, for those with the ears to hear them. But it was no longer acceptable to just say them out loud. White Christian nationalism seemed kinder and gentler. Though not of course to those on the receiving end.

Its individualist strand underwent a similar evolution during this period. The market replaced the frontier as the arena of "freedom."[58] The maintenance of order at home and abroad was transferred from lynch mobs and posses to the police and the uniformed military. Christian morality was shrunk down to fit into the box of "personal accountability." Scouts, slave drivers, and cowboys were out; soldiers, entrepreneurs, and sports heroes were in. This despite, or rather because of, growing economic inequality, mass incarceration of Black men, and the growth of the Religious Right.

By the early aughts, American politics seemed to have settled into a predictable equilibrium. The country was closely divided and elections were ritual tugs-of-war between two evenly matched teams fighting over marginal tax rates and Social Security spending. The team leaders were generally polite to one another. Al Gore conceded a close and controversial election to George W. Bush. John McCain memorably defended Barack Obama against conspiracist claims that he was a "secret Muslim." George and Laura Bush welcomed the first Black president and first lady to the White House following McCain's defeat.

But the surface calm proved deceptive. Deeper down, the tectonic plates of American history were grinding against one another. The pressure and the heat were building. The first sign of trouble was the election of 2016. The next was the violent eruption on January 6, 2021. It turned out that white Christian nationalism had not weakened or disappeared. On the contrary, it was gaining strength and changing shape. Yet again.

# Chapter 3

# Freedom, Violence, Order

On February 19, 2009, roughly one month after the inauguration of America's first Black president, Rick Santelli, a financial reporter with CNBC, delivered an on-air rant from the trading floor of the Chicago Mercantile Exchange. Blaming the 2008 financial crisis on "losers" who had taken out mortgages they couldn't afford, he excoriated the new president for bailing them out. "This is America!" he shouted, "If you read our Founding Fathers, people like Benjamin Franklin and Jefferson, what we're doing in this country now is making them roll over in their graves." He then called for the formation of "another Tea Party" to resist federal taxation and defend individual rights. It was dubbed "the rant heard round the world."

On January 20, 2017, a little less than eight years later, Donald Trump was inaugurated as the 45th president of the United States. The focus of his campaign had not been on defending individual rights so much as restoring national greatness. Under his leadership, Trump promised, "[t]he American people" would "take back [their] country." They would "band together . . . around Christianity." They would "start winning again" and "saying Merry Christmas again" and "bring [Christianity] back because it's a good thing." They would also put "America first," restore "law and order," build a "great wall" around the nation to keep out "criminals" and "illegals," and institute a "total and complete shutdown of all Muslims entering the United States." Trump exchanged the dog whistles for a bullhorn, leaving little doubt about his agenda. Making America "great again" seemed to mean making it both whiter and more Christian.

On March 12, 2021, a year into the COVID pandemic, the Republican senator from Wisconsin, Ron Johnson, reflected on the two defining political events of the tumultuous year gone by: the Capitol insurrection on January 6 and the Black Lives Matter protests of 2020. Johnson said that he "wasn't concerned" about the insurrectionists, because "those were people that love this country, that truly respect law enforcement [and] would never do anything to break the law." "Now, had the tables been turned," he mused, "and those were tens of thousands of Black Lives Matter and Antifa protesters, I might have been a little concerned." It was a strange claim, given that the insurrectionists *did* break the law, that many of them violently assaulted the Capitol police, and that a few seemingly had plans to execute members of Congress. Of course, some Black Lives Matter and Antifa protesters had also clashed with police and destroyed property the previous summer. But they did not attempt to overturn a presidential election.

Apart from the fact that these three messages were all delivered by conservative white men, they would seem to have little in common. The first two even seem somewhat at odds: Santelli's diatribe seemed to connect America's founders into libertarians; Trump's campaign centered on religious identity and ethno-nationalism. The text of Johnson's remarks concerned violence; but the subtext was of course race.

This chapter will show how these three messages, the men who conveyed them, and the events they describe, are connected to one another. We are not the only ones to note the link. Political scientists Jacob Hacker and Paul Pierson have also emphasized the connection between economic libertarianism, ethno-nationalism, and violent racial animus.[1] But their explanation focuses on wealthy economic elites who manipulate the masses for their own benefit. This is part of the story, to be sure, but it is not the whole story. Conservative religious leaders also played an important part. And both were sowing their seeds in a rich soil fertilized by three centuries of white Christian nationalism. The Tea Party, the MAGA movement, and the Capitol insurrection all sprouted from this same soil. These three movements are, in fact, just three chapters in one story—the ongoing story of white Christian nationalism in America.

The leading role in the deep story is typically played by a white Christian man of a certain sort: aggressive but disciplined, ready to use violence to defend (his) "freedom" and impose "law and order" (on others). Think John Wayne—or Donald Trump.[2] Or, for that matter, Sarah Palin or Marjorie Taylor Greene. Sometimes, women who embrace traditionally masculine activities (e.g., shooting guns or lifting weights) can also be cast in the male lead.

As we saw in Chapter 2, a certain kind of individualism has been a key part of white Christian nationalism right from the start. The Puritan warrior is an early example. He built a "city on a hill"—and burned native settlements. Later examples include the Christian slaveholder who ruled with a mixture of paternal benevolence and brutal violence; or the Christian homesteader who settled the frontier and drove out the natives; the WASP imperialist who selflessly pursued his self-interest overseas; or the Cold War evangelical who battled "godless communism." They, too, were prepared to use violence to defend (their) liberty and impose law and order (on others).

The more recent strain of individualism within white Christian nationalism is what we and our fellow sociologist Gerardo Marti have called "Christian libertarianism."[3] Having emerged during the middle decades of the 20th century, its motto is "personal account-ability." It presumes that one's lot in life is a result of one's personal choices—and only those choices. Historical and social contexts are irrelevant. Wealth or poverty, salvation or damnation, bliss or de-spair—it's all up to you! But . . . you will also be held accountable for your choices, in this life and the next, either by the market or by God. Christian libertarianism joined free markets, racial purity, and authoritarian religion into a unified "Biblical worldview."[4] That worldview is very much alive if not altogether well.


## THE TEA PARTY: LIBERTARIANISM? WHITE CHRISTIAN NATIONALISM? OR BOTH?

On April 15, 2009, hundreds of thousands of demonstrators in hundreds of cities across America participated in the first major Tea Party protest. The date was chosen for a reason: April 15 is "tax day," the deadline for submitting individual tax returns to the IRS. The "Tea Party" label was also significant. The original Boston Tea Party of 1773 was a protest against the British tax on tea exports to the American colonies. The Tea Party presented itself as a libertarian movement against high taxes and government overreach.

Much of the rhetoric and symbolism at the April 15th demonstrations was in fact libertarian in tone. Some speakers denounced the government-funded financial bailout known as the "Troubled Asset Relief Program" or TARP. Later, they would focus their ire on the Affordable Care Act, a.k.a, "Obamacare." Others explained that "TEA" stands for "taxed enough already." Some hung tea bags from their glasses or hats. Many displayed "Gadsden flags," the iconic, yellow Revolutionary era flag emblazoned with the words "Don't Tread on Me" and an image of a rattlesnake ready to strike.

But some of the rhetoric and symbolism did not fit so neatly into a libertarian frame. At a rally on Boston Common, for example, Michael Johns of the Heritage Foundation and cofounder of the Tea Party movement announced to his audience "Mr. Obama . . . said this is not a Christian nation," eliciting loud boos. Then he addressed the president directly in his speech: "Mr. Obama, every historical document signed in Philadelphia, every founding document of this nation, has cited our creator . . . that is the foundation of our liberties and our god-given freedoms. AND THEY ARE GOD GIVEN FREEDOMS. A nation that denies its creator, and rejects its principles will not long endure."[5] Christian symbols were often on display at other rallies that day. In Oklahoma City, one of the protesters hoisted a sign proclaiming "One Nation under God."[6] Racist rhetoric was not uncommon either. In Fort Myers, Florida, two protesters proclaimed that Obama was a "puppet" of Jewish bankers.[7] Tricorn hats and other colonial garb were frequent attire. Some cosplayers dressed up as Revolutionary soldiers. The messages, in other words, were not purely libertarian. They were also white, Christian, and nationalist.

As academics and journalists began researching the Tea Party supporters, they made several important discoveries.[8] The movement did mobilize a fair number of younger, secular libertarians. So, the libertarian label was not entirely misleading. But as sociologists Ruth Braunstein and Malaena Taylor have shown, roughly half of Tea Partiers self-identify as "born-again or evangelical Christians" and well over half (57%) believe that America "is currently and has always been a Christian nation,"—a greater percentage than even self-identified members of the Religious Right.[9] Yet when it comes to measures of personal religiosity like church attendance, Tea Partiers score far lower. In other words, the myth of a Christian nation was far more important to them than Christianity itself.

"Christian" instead functions as a cultural identity marker, one that separates "us" from "them." As one would expect, the libertarian-minded Tea Partiers supported free markets and opposed government programs. But so do their more devout evangelical allies. The movement was composed of (culturally) Christian libertarians and (economically) libertarian Christians.[10] Their only real points of disagreement were "social" issues, like sexual morality.

What was true at the grassroots level was also true at the commanding heights of the new movement. Local Tea Party groups were generously supported by conservative business interests. In this case, the Koch Brothers' libertarian-leaning "Americans for Prosperity" didn't hesitate to "spread the wealth around." Evangelical political activists were also quick to show their support. Ralph Reed formed his "Faith and Freedom Coalition" to support the Tea Party movement (and reboot his career following a damaging corruption scandal).

The Tea Party was fueled by a blend of big money and popular energy. But ethnic and racial anxiety were the spark plugs that really ignited it.[11] The very thought of a Black man in the White House was deeply disturbing to many white Americans. Running a close second was the fear of religious and cultural marginalization by radical leftists, secularists, or Muslims. Before his election, controversy swirled about Obama's connection with Black nationalism and liberation theology following video footage of sermons from Obama's former pastor, Jeremiah Wright. Former vice-presidential nominee Sarah Palin warned supporters, "This is not a man who sees America as you and I see it," and then accused Obama of "pallin' around with terrorists." After Obama's election, Donald Trump famously insisted that the new president was not born in the United States (a public obsession that would put the businessman and reality TV star in the political limelight). Others whispered that the president was a "secret Muslim." Right-wing shock-jock and Tea Party champion Rush Limbaugh composed and performed a song called "Barack the Magic Negro," sung to the tune of "Puff the Magic Dragon." Opinion polls found high levels of racial animus among Tea Party supporters, and Tea Party demonstrations were awash with anti-Obama caricatures. Some painted a Hitler mustache on Obama's face. Others put a turban on his head. Unsurprisingly, in Braunstein and Taylor's 2017 study, one of the strongest predictors of Tea Party membership was contempt for Obama.

Nativist sentiment was also widespread among Tea Partiers. In part, this was due to the infiltration of the movement by anti-immigrant vigilante groups such as the "Minutemen," which dispatched armed "patrols" to the US-Mexico border.[12] But anti-immigrant sentiment was hardly a fringe phenomenon within the GOP, as the ferocious backlash against the immigration reforms proposed by President George W. Bush in 2007 made abundantly clear.

The connection is confirmed by the opinion polls. They showed a strong correlation between support for the Tea Party and opposition to immigration. A 2015 poll conducted by the Public Religion Research Institute, for example, found that among whites who held a "very favorable" opinion of the Tea Party, 70% or more believed that America's economic struggles were due to undocumented immigrants taking American jobs; that immigrants (not just undocumented ones) had negative effects on jobs, housing, and health care; and that it bothered them when they met an immigrant who didn't speak English.

One of the more distinctive features of the Tea Party movement was its constant appeals to, and religious reverence for, the US Constitution. Tea Partiers believed that the "founding fathers" had established a "limited government" whose only purpose was to protect "individual liberties." They often pointed to the 10th Amendment, according to which "powers not delegated to the United States . . . are reserved to the States . . . or to the people." Tea Party leaders such as Texas Senator Ted Cruz often styled themselves as "Constitutional conservatives." Members of the rank and file sometimes carried pocket-sized copies of the Constitution; many joined study groups where they parsed and memorized passages from the Constitution. Despite the fact that there were often sharp disagreements about the meaning of the Constitution among legal scholars, Tea Partiers insisted that its meaning was clear to anyone with eyes. To secular observers, these practices probably seemed very odd. To those who knew the evangelical subculture, they were all too familiar. Pocket Bibles, Bible study groups, and biblical literalism were among its defining elements. Conservative white evangelicals simply applied them to another sacred text: the US Constitution.

It is little surprise, then, that in November 2020, roughly 70% of white evangelicals we surveyed believed the US Constitution is divinely inspired, nearly 80% affirmed constitutional "originalism," and over three-quarters reject the idea that the Constitution should be regularly amended to account for cultural changes. Moreover, these views sacralizing the founding documents correspond with free-market, libertarian views. For instance, Figure 3.1 shows how three beliefs about the US Constitution correspond with white Americans indicating they have "serious moral problems with socialism," the perennial bogeyman of Tea Partiers and conservatives more broadly. Clearly, the more whites affirm the US Constitution's divine inspiration, unchanging character, and originalist interpretation (all evocative of biblicist Christianity), the more likely they are to reject socialism on moral grounds.

The libertarian ideas of the Tea Party movement were entangled with the ethno-traditionalist impulses of white Christian nationalism.

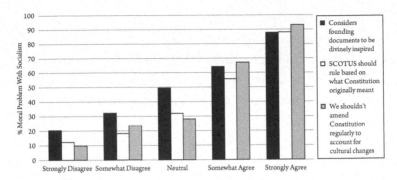

Figure 3.1. Percentage of white Americans who have serious moral problems with socialism across their agreement with views sacralizing the US Constitution. *Source:* *Public Discourse and Ethics Survey (Wave 6; November 2020)*

## "MAGA!" THE SECULARIZATION OF WHITE CHRISTIAN NATIONALISM

How could conservative evangelicals who claimed to defend "family values," "character," and "civility" support a thrice-married, egomaniacal real-estate mogul who paid off porn stars? Outside observers have been asking some version of this question ever since Trump's early victories in the 2016 Republican presidential primaries. So have some elite insiders, shocked to discover that their church and their party were not what they thought they were, at least not anymore.

The answer is complicated.

The first thing to note is that Trump's MAGA narrative can be understood as a semi-secularized version of white Christian nationalism's deep story. Trump's narrative is shorn of the sorts of biblical references and allusions that peppered earlier presidents' speeches. But the MAGA narrative still has many parallels with the deep story. The most obvious one is between the apocalyptic strand of white Christian nationalism and the catastrophizing aspect of MAGA. Premillennialists believe that there will be a final battle between good and evil, a life-and-death struggle between natural and supernatural forces that is visible to them, but invisible to unbelievers. Trump's worldview is similar. "Disaster" is one of his favorite words. He sees life as an endless battle between us and them. He sees hidden conspiracies everywhere he looks. We should not be surprised that Trump's rhetoric resonated so strongly with many white devotees of Christian nationalism. Their deep stories are quite similar.

If self-identified evangelicals respond to Trump's semi-secularized version of white Christian nationalism, then this is in part because the evangelical label itself has become semi-secularized as well. Political scientist Ryan Burge has shown that an increasing number of Americans outside of evangelical Protestant traditions (such as Catholics, Mormons, Eastern Orthodox Christians, Jews, and even Muslims and Hindus) are now identifying as "evangelical or born-again Christians." He shows that this is largely driven by the merging of Republican and evangelical identities, so that when Americans are asked whether they're "evangelical," they increasingly read this not as a question about their theological beliefs, but whether they identify with the Republican Party.

The MAGA narrative is not only a secularized white Christian nationalism; it is a reactionary version. In the Puritans' Promised Land narrative, recall, blood was the master metaphor that linked blood belonging (race), blood sacrifice (religion), and blood conquest (nation). In the sanitized 20th-century version of white Christian nationalism known as "American exceptionalism," the blood metaphors were diluted into polite euphemisms such as "ultimate sacrifice." In Trump's "politically incorrect" version, blood reappeared. Sometimes it did so explicitly, as in the apocryphal story about "Muslim terrorists" executed with "bullets dipped in pig's blood" that he often worked into his stump speech.[13] Given the importance of blood sacrifice in many versions of Christian theology, and the mystical powers often attributed to it, Trump's blood rhetoric probably resonated with many.

More often, though, Trump's blood metaphors were implicit. Amid the firestorm ignited by his remarks about "undesirable" immigrants from "shithole countries," for instance, Trump wondered aloud why there were not more new arrivals from Norway.[14] As noted in Chapter 2, "Nordics" were the whitest of whites in the racial hierarchies of early 20th-century America. Not since the days of Teddy Roosevelt and Woodrow Wilson had an American president spoken this way. The message was likely not lost on Trump's white nationalist fans.

Even Trump's two signature issues—the "Muslim ban" and the border wall—can be read through the blood metaphor. With the "closing of the frontier," the United States had largely achieved its "manifest destiny" of continental expansion. The internal frontier became an external border, the outer skin of the national body, as it were. It was crucial that the national body not be penetrated or polluted by non-white or non-Christian bodies. Especially not the bodies of "Mexican rapists" and "Muslim terrorists" who would seek to contaminate or destroy the national body. In this sense, the ban and the wall were both meant to protect the pure blood of the national body from pollution or infection.

MAGA was white Christian nationalism shorn of biblical references, but with the same deep story. "Disaster" replaced "apocalypse." Broken promises to the "forgotten man" replaced a broken covenant with the Puritans' God. Though race, religion, and nation were still tightly entangled, both in the equation of "Muslim/Arab/

terrorist" and of "white/evangelical/patriot." There was nothing subtle about it. Trump and his followers reveled in "saying the quiet part out loud" as a way of "owning the libs." Audiences cheered Trump's "honest" talk about "shithole countries," "pig's blood," and "banging heads." Not since George Wallace had a presidential candidate spoken this way. Not since Woodrow Wilson had such an outspoken racist occupied the White House.

## FREEDOM, VIOLENCE, ORDER I: TRUMPISM AND CHRISTIAN LIBERTARIANISM

Many critics regard John Ford's 1956 movie, *The Searchers*, as the greatest Western ever made. It opens, as many Westerns do, with a lone gunman riding his horse through the iconic landscape of Monument Valley.[15] The gunman in question is none other than John Wayne, the man who defined American masculinity for the post-WWII generation. Wayne plays Ethan Edwards, a Confederate veteran returning home to West Texas after fighting in the Civil War, and the Mexican War before that. He sports a Winchester repeater and Colt revolver (iconic weapons that postdate those wars by several decades). Shortly thereafter, Ethan's brother, sister-in-law, and nephew are killed by Comanche raiders, and his two young nieces taken captive. Ethan sets out to find them, encountering—and killing—many natives along the way. Having accomplished his mission after five long years, Ethan rides back into the desert, alone. Ford's movie, released just two years after the *Brown v. Board* decision, may have been intended as a critique of white racism. But that is not how it was sold and probably not how it was received either. With the usual hyperbole, theater posters described it as "the biggest, roughest, toughest, most beautiful movie ever made." A white man using lethal violence to rescue a white girl from racial others while roaming the desert landscape of "Indian territory," a place seemingly devoid of history and civilization, to restore order to his family—it is hard to imagine a more condensed depiction of white masculine mythology in modern-day America.

But where is Christianity in all of this? It is a question that has haunted many Christian men, as historian Kristin Kobes Du Mez explains in her bestselling book, *Jesus and John Wayne.*[16] Part of the problem was Jesus. He was, perhaps, a bit of a loner. But he did not carry a weapon or die in a blaze of glory. Nor did he have a wife or family. He was given to occasional displays of righteous anger— there was that incident with the money changers in the temple. But he mostly preached love, peace, and forgiveness, not the hate, war, and vengeance pursued by Ethan Edwards and other fictional representations of white American manhood.

The other problem was white manhood itself. It was in crisis. It had been in crisis for some time. (Perhaps it is always "in crisis.") White men now lived in teeming cities and towns, worked in crowded offices and factories, and bought their food in shops and supermarkets. But the more comfortable they got, the more they yearned for open spaces, free movement, and existential challenges.[17] And so they found new frontiers in business, free spaces in "the great outdoors," and competitive challenges in sports. In John Wayne, they found a fantasy of masculine fulfillment.

But what, to paraphrase, hath Jesus to do with John Wayne? In many corners of white evangelicalism, the answer is this: a great deal. John Wayne could not be made into Jesus, so Jesus was made into John Wayne. Not "a wuss who took a beating and spent a lot of time putting product in his hair," as one popular preacher explained; nor a "neutered and limp-wristed popular Sky Fairy," in another's words. Instead, Jesus became tall and strong, fair and handsome, a warrior and fighter, a leader and an entrepreneur, in word as well as deed. He became, in effect, Straight White American Super Jesus.[18] A Jesus who doesn't bring peace, but openly carries a sword. A Jesus who kicks down the cross and thrashes the (socialist) money changers. White masculinity, American individualism, and Christian libertarianism all rolled into one.

Which brings us back to Donald Trump. Trumpism has been called many things: populism, patriarchalism, nationalism, and even fascism. All of these labels capture something about the Trump phenomenon. But only one of them—patriarchalism—hints at the connection to individualism. And yet, it is there—and powerfully so. MAGA is a secularized and reactionary form of white Christian nationalism. Which makes Donald Trump the new John Wayne. (Though he is more often portrayed as the new Rambo, the rogue special forces soldier played by Sylvester Stallone.)

So why does Trump's ethos still resonate with so many white Christians? Because there are many deep continuities between Trumpism and white Christian nationalism's core ideals of freedom, order, and violence. Or, in story form: (white) men exercising (righteous) violence to defend (their) freedom and impose (racial and gender) order. Viewed through this lens, it becomes easier to understand Trump's hold over many white Christian men. He is a cruder version of their masculine ideal.

Let's begin with "freedom." When criticized for his intemperate language—the insults, threats, and profanity—Trump and his supporters style themselves as defenders of "free speech" and opponents of "cancel culture" who dare to be "politically incorrect." In other words, they claim the God-given right to use racist and sexist language with impunity, as in the "good old days" of Jim Crow and "Mad Men." Little surprise, then, that in our surveys over three-quarters of white voters who rejected politically correct speech and felt "too many people are easily offended these days over language" voted for Trump in 2016 and then again in 2020.

But the "freedom" rhetoric is more than just a reaction to political correctness. Political scientist Andrew Lewis has documented what he calls "the rights turn" in conservative Christian politics.[19] Increasingly, over the course of several decades, Lewis shows, religious conservatives backed away from justifying opposition to sexual, gender, or ethnic minorities on explicitly moral or religious grounds. Those arguments don't play so well anymore in a post-Christian society. Religious freedom is an important right. But some Christian conservatives now bend the language of "free speech," or "religious freedom," or "religious liberty" into a cudgel that can be used to deny minority grievances—and privilege their own.

The 2020 election was a prime example of this sort of language deployed in opposition to minority claims. Trump promised that the Democrats and Biden, in particular, would eviscerate Americans' First and Second Amendment rights. In an August 6, 2020, speech, for example, Trump warned that Biden was "following the radical left agenda. Take away your guns, destroy your Second Amendment. No religion, no anything, hurt the Bible, hurt God . . . He's against God. He's against guns."[20] In the immediate context of 2020, religious freedoms also included freedom to disregard mask-wearing mandates or social distancing orders to meet in religious services. But "religious liberty" has also historically meant liberty for Christian businesses to refuse coverage for abortions, deny service to LGBTQ persons, or for pastors to denounce them openly from the pulpit, or for Christian adoption agencies that take federal money to deny service to anyone but evangelical Christians.

Just after the November 2020 election, we asked Americans to indicate how important various issues were to their voting decision. Roughly 68% of those who said religious freedom was a "very important" influence on their vote pulled the lever for Trump. And among those who said religious freedom was "the most important" issue influencing their vote, nearly 95% voted for Trump. But does this language mean "religious freedom" in an inclusive sense that would favor government neutrality on the issue of religion? Not at all. Panel A in Figure 3.2 shows that even after accounting for relevant characteristics, it is Americans who want to elevate and institutionalize (white) Christianity's influence in the public square who prioritized "religious freedom."[21]

Notably, Panel B shows that white Americans who felt Christians faced considerable discrimination these days and that transgender persons were *not* discriminated against were also more likely to prioritize "religious freedom" in their 2020 vote. In other words, not only is the language of "religious liberty" or "religious freedom" dog-whistle language for conservative Christian supremacy, it also reflects a belief that Christians are the true victims in American society. Their idea of "freedom" means "freedom for us."

But, what of "them"?

This is where violence comes in. Trump, himself, does not employ physical violence. However, he is a master of verbal violence, skilled at using words as weapons to wound his opponents and intimidate his rivals. "Crooked Hillary," "Sleepy Joe," "Lyin' Ted," "Little Marco," "Low Energy Jeb." Just as the Western hero uses bullets to take out "Indians," so Trump fires off epithets to take out "RINOs" and "leftists" to the delight of his fans. Of course, Trump is not above threatening or inciting physical violence. "I could stand in the middle of Fifth Avenue and shoot somebody, and I wouldn't lose any voters," he boasted in early 2016. Confronted with protesters on the campaign trail, he urged his supporters to "punch them in the face" or "knock the crap out of them." "Don't be nice about it," he added, "I'll pay for your lawyer."[22]

**Panel A: Christians Nationalism**

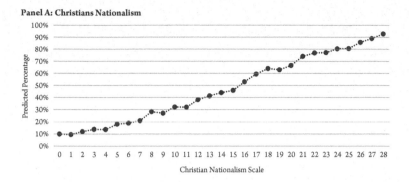

**Panel B: Discrimination Against Christians and Transgender Persons**

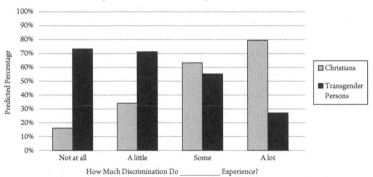

Figure 3.2. Predicted percentage of whites who said "religious freedom" was a "very important" influence on their 2020 presidential election vote across Christian nationalism and their belief that Christians and Transgender Persons are discriminated against.

*Note:* Binary logistic regression (1 = religious freedom "very important," 0 = other response) with Christian nationalism scale, discrimination against Christians, Muslims, Atheists, Jews, and Trans* persons, controlling for age, gender, education, income, political party identification, political ideology, religious tradition, religiosity, and region.

*Source: Public Discourse and Ethics Survey (Wave 6; November 2020)*

But how exactly is the sort of white Christian nationalism Trump endorsed and that so many of his supporters internalize connected to displays of violence like the murder of unarmed Black men or the Capitol insurrection? Or for that matter things like guns, capital punishment, or torture? To answer that question, we also need to understand the vital connection between white Christian nationalism, violence, and social order, or to put it more bluntly, the link between white Christian nationalism and authoritarian control over outsiders: Freedom for "us"; violence and order for "them."

## FREEDOM, VIOLENCE, ORDER II: BLACK LIVES MATTER VS. THE CAPITOL INSURRECTION

The death of George Floyd at the hands of Derek Chauvin, a white police officer, on May 25, 2020, ignited a wave of national protest such as the nation had not seen since the late 1960s. The overwhelming majority of the protesters were peaceful. But a small minority clashed with police and engaged in rioting and looting. White vigilantes and armed militias appeared at some protests on the pretense of aiding the police and protecting private property. On August 25, 2020, exactly three months after Floyd's death, a 17-year old white man named Kyle Rittenhouse had his mother drive him from Antioch, Illinois, to Kenosha, Wisconsin. By the end of the evening, Rittenhouse had killed two people with an assault rifle and wounded another. Trump applauded him. And the Republican base crowdfunded his bail and legal defense.

When Chauvin was found guilty of murdering George Floyd, the reaction was very different. Fox News Host Tucker Carlson described the trial as "an attack on civilization." Christian Right blogger and author of the 2020 book *Church of Cowards: A Wake-Up Call to Complacent Christians*, Matt Walsh tweeted, "A few years ago, George Floyd forced his way into a woman's home and robbed her at gunpoint. Today, that woman has to watch as millions turn her victimizer into their messiah. We are a sick country." And he immediately added, "The only systemic and institutional racism left in America is anti-white racism."[23]

These two examples are part of a larger pattern. Conservative whites fear and abhor violence in some contexts (for example, from Blacks, immigrants, or Muslims). But they applaud it in other contexts (for instance, by police, soldiers, and other "good guys with guns"). The key that explains the inconsistency, we argue, is white Christian nationalism and its racialized combination of libertarian freedom (for whites) and authoritarian control (over non-whites).

In February 2021, we asked Americans a series of questions about the appropriate use of violence. Several questions were more about violence in general. Panel A in Figure 3.3 shows whites' predicted agreement with statements like "I am against all forms of violence," or "A world without any violence is a goal we should all work toward," or "Authorities should always prefer to talk out problems rather than resort to physical violence." We plot these values across our Christian nationalism scale. What should be clear is that Christian nationalism doesn't seem to be strongly associated with white Americans' views about violence in general. To be sure, as white Americans affirm Christian nationalism, their agreement with these anti-violence statements declines slightly. But it's only slightly. In other words, we can't conclude that white Christian nationalism somehow strongly endorses violence for its own sake, at least not after we account for factors like conservative political ideology, partisanship, or age. But what happens when we consider violence used by authorities or at least "good guys" for the betterment of society, perhaps to control problem populations?

Panel B allows us to observe white Americans' predicted agreement with various statements about what we could call "righteous violence," where ostensibly threatening or violent "bad guys" or "evil doers" are handled with violence in response. As before, we

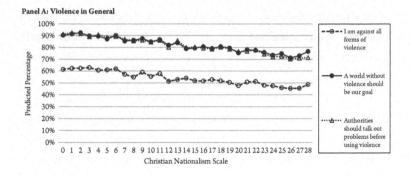

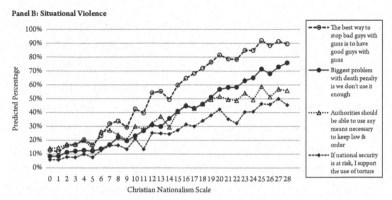

Figure 3.3. Whites' predicted agreement with views about violence across Christian nationalism.

**Note:** Binary logistic regression (1 = Agree, 0 = Other) with Christian nationalism scale, controlling for age, gender, education, income, political party identification, political ideology, religious tradition, religiosity, and region.

**Source:** *Public Discourse and Ethics Survey (Wave 7; February 2021)*

plot the predicted values across white Americans' scores on our Christian nationalism scale. Though white Christian nationalism was only weakly related with white Americans' views toward violence in general, here it is not only associated with support for "righteous violence," but it is far and away the strongest predictor in each of our models. The more that white Americans seek to institutionalize "Christian values" or the nation's Christian identity, the more strongly they support gun-toting good guys taking on (real or imagined) gun-toting bad guys, the more frequent use of the death penalty, any-means-necessary policing, and even torture as an inter-rogation technique.

Why the strong connection? And why wasn't white Christian nationalism associated with generalized violence in the same way? We've already observed that the "individualism" or "libertarianism" associated with white Christian nationalism inclines Americans to claim "freedom" or "liberty" for themselves. And traditionally this has involved restricting the liberty of gender, sexual, or racial minorities. White Christian nationalism designates who is "worthy" of the freedom it cherishes, namely, "people like us." But for the "others" outside that group, white Christian nationalism grants whites in authority the "freedom" to control such populations, to maintain a certain kind of social order that privileges "good people like us" through violence if necessary.[24]

Other than violence against Black Americans in the criminal jus-tice system, perhaps no two contemporary situations demonstrate this "us vs. them" dynamic of liberty and "righteous violence" than Americans' current understanding of (1) "worthiness" to partici-pate in democracy and (2) the Capitol insurrection.

Both legal and illegal voter suppression have long been a tactic of white conservatives to tilt elections in their favor. Yet political scientists and sociologists often forget the ideological support for such efforts since the civil rights movement has come from white Christian nationalism. Just months before the 1980 election, Paul Weyrich, cofounder of the American Legislative Exchange Council and the Moral Majority, spoke at a Dallas conference to an audience that included evangelical leaders such as Tim LaHaye, Pat Robertson, James Robison, and W. A. Criswell, as well as GOP presidential can-didate Ronald Reagan.[25] Weyrich told his audience, "Now many of our Christians have what I call the 'goo-goo syndrome.' Good government. They want everybody to vote. I don't want everybody to vote. Elections are not won by a majority of people. They never have been from the beginning of our country, and they are not now." He went on, explaining: "As a matter of fact, our leverage in the elections quite candidly goes up as the voting populace goes down." Here before his Christian Right audience, Weyrich explained the strategy: our group stays in power if fewer people—especially our opponents—are able to vote. The policy implication is clear: make it harder for "problem" populations to vote, or at least don't make it easier.

Weyrich's antidemocratic sentiment has been repeated on the Christian Right for decades since. Also among those in attendance at that 1980 meeting was longtime conservative activist Phyllis Schlafly. Leading up to the 2012 presidential election, Schlafly underscored why limiting early voting was so critical. "The reduction in the number of days allowed for early voting is particularly important because early voting plays a major role in Obama's ground game. The Democrats carried most states that allow many days of early voting." And several years later, former Baptist pastor, governor of Arkansas, and GOP presidential candidate Mike Huckabee echoed Weyrich's words: "I know that most politicians say we want everyone to vote, I'm gonna be honest with you, I don't want everyone to vote. If they're so stupid—that's right, if they're gonna vote for me they need to vote, if they're not gonna vote for me they need to stay home. I mean, it's that simple . . . But in the big picture, there are people who vote and they have no idea what our Constitution says."[26] This last part of Huckabee's quote is instructive in that he ties citizens' worthiness to vote not only to their support for him, but to their knowledge of the Constitution.

Undergirding these views is an understanding of democratic participation that has deep historical roots, namely, that only certain groups (i.e., people like us) are "worthy" to have a say in government and it is perfectly acceptable to make it more difficult to vote, and particularly for those who might be "undeserving" (i.e., people like them). Indeed, we find the connection between white Christian nationalism and these attitudes is exceptionally strong.

In October 2020, just before the election, we asked Americans a series of questions about voter access. Figure 3.4 shows how white Americans' views change across their adherence to Christian nationalist ideology. Even after accounting for political partisanship and conservative political ideology along with other relevant characteristics, Christian nationalism is the strongest predictor that white Americans believe we already make it too easy to vote in this country and that they would support hypothetical laws restricting the vote from certain felons or only to those who could pass a basic civics test—a shocking echo of Jim Crow. By contrast, as white Americans' affirmation of our Christian nationalism indicators increases, their likelihood of believing voter suppression in presidential elections is a real problem plummets. Why would we see these patterns even after we account for relevant political characteristics? Because white Christian nationalism is fundamentally antidemocratic for "others," that is, those who are "unworthy" of participation. This is how order is maintained: freedom for us, restraint for them.

Violence related to democratic participation was far more widespread before the civil rights movement, when it was commonplace for Southern whites to intimidate or brutalize minorities who wanted to cast a vote. But antidemocratic violence was resurrected with a vengeance on January 6, 2021. Leading up to the 2020 election, Donald Trump assured his followers that the increase in mail-in ballots and early voting related to COVID-19 would lead to massive voter fraud. In a May 26 Tweet, for example, he warned,

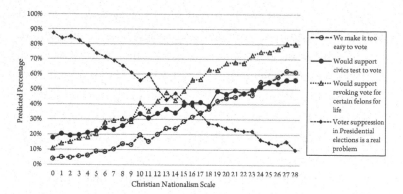

Figure 3.4.  Predicted percentage of white Americans who affirm statements on voter access across Christian nationalism.

**Note:** Binary logistic regression (1 = Agree, 0 = Other) with Christian nationalism scale, controlling for age, gender, education, income, political party identification, political ideology, religious tradition, religiosity, and region.

**Source:** *Public Discourse and Ethics Survey (Wave 5; October 2020)*

"There is NO WAY (ZERO!) that Mail-In Ballots will be anything less than substantially fraudulent. Mailboxes will be robbed, ballots will be forged & even illegally printed out & fraudulently signed." He continued this narrative right up to November 8. And as it became clear that he would lose the Electoral College vote, Trump ramped up his Tweets, repeatedly making baseless and thoroughly debunked claims that the entire election had been rigged and that he had actually won in a landslide. This narrative was either repeated explicitly by his Christian nationalist supporters like Eric Metaxas, Charlie Kirk, Jenna Ellis, Michele Bachmann, and virtually the entire lineup on American Family Radio, or it was more subtly repeated with talk of "unanswered questions," and "discrepancies" by supporters like Mike Huckabee, Tony Perkins, Robert Jeffress, or Franklin Graham. Lies about a stolen election were also stoked by Republican congressmen and bolstered by a collective move to refuse confirming election results. Then came January 6th.

We won't recount the horrifying chaos, fear, and violence at the Capitol. Written accounts, video footage, and reconstructions abound. Historian Peter Manseau has cataloged the collage of Christian symbols, flags, prayers, T-shirts, and language under the Twitter hashtag #CapitolSiegeReligion. It was a display of white Christian nationalism so blatant and horrifying that even Trump-supporting evangelicals like Al Mohler had to acknowledge it, while quickly dismissing it as fringe.

But it is not fringe. In February 2021, roughly one month after the insurrection, we surveyed Americans about the events of January 6th. Unsurprisingly, the more that white Americans affirmed white Christian nationalist ideology, the more likely they were to deny Trump had anything to do with the event (see Figure 3.5). Instead, they blamed the violence on Black Lives Matter or Antifa. At the same time, the more whites affirm Christian nationalism, the more likely they are to say they stand with the rioters and the less likely

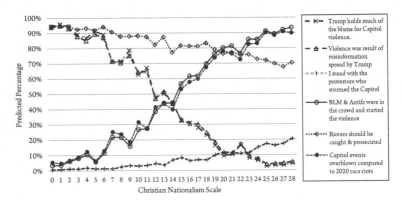

Figure 3.5. Predicted percentage of white Americans who hold various views about the Capitol insurrection across Christian nationalism.

**Note:** Binary logistic regression (1 = Agree, 0 = Other) with Christian nationalism scale, controlling for age, gender, education, income, political party identification, political ideology, religious tradition, religiosity, and region.

**Source:** *Public Discourse and Ethics Survey (Wave 7; February 2021)*

they are to say that the rioters should all be caught and prosecuted. But if the violence was caused by Antifa and BLM, why would these white Americans (who absolve Trump of all blame) be more likely to stand with the rioters and object to them being caught and prosecuted?

What is going on here? One possibility is that white Christian nationalists acknowledge that angry white Christians were engaged in violence at the Capitol, but that their violence was righteous and justified and should not be prosecuted. It was justified, because it was a response to much worse violence by Black Lives Matter and Antifa protesters the previous summer. In this, they are simply following the logic of the deep story: "This is our country, not theirs. And we are at liberty to take it back by violence."

## CONCLUSION

White Christian nationalism is a theory of order, and of hierarchy. It distinguishes insiders and outsiders, and when those two must occupy the same country, those on top and those on the bottom. "People like us"—white Christian citizens—are the true Americans. Everyone else is only here on their sufferance. In the blunt language of the Trump-friendly Claremont Institute: "most people living in the United States today—certainly more than half—are not Americans in any meaningful sense of the term." They are "zombies" and "rodents," not "real men and women who love truth and beauty."[27]

White Christian nationalism is also a theory of freedom. White Christian citizens have God-given rights, rights to "life, liberty, and property" in John Locke's words or "life, liberty, and the pursuit of happiness" in Jefferson's reformulation. These rights are "inalienable" and "inviolable." They are not granted by the government; nor can they be taken away, or even encroached on, by the same. They are "sacred." No one may violate them. Especially not someone from another tribe.

Which brings us to our third theme—violence. It connects order and freedom. Violence can be a source of order but also of disorder. It can be an expression of freedom but also an assault on freedom. It all depends on who is engaging in violence. Violence can be understood as an attempt to maintain proper order when (implicitly white) police or "good guys with guns" wield it against (implicitly non-white) "bad guys." It can even be read as an attempt to restore order as in the Capitol insurrection. But it is viewed as moral degradation and dystopian chaos when attributed to Black Lives Matter, Antifa, or the inhabitants of inner cities. White violence is the ultimate source of order; Black or leftist violence, by contrast, is the ultimate source of disorder. White Christian violence is also the most fundamental expression of freedom; the violence of minorities or perceived socialists, on the other hand, is the deepest threat to freedom. "Good people," another high-minded Claremont author explained, must be "dangerous people," which is to say, white "patriots" ready to use violence against Latino gangs and Black criminals. This is what passes for "political philosophy" in the MAGAverse.[28]

# Chapter 4

# Avoiding "The Big One"

It is tempting to dismiss the insurrection as an isolated incident perpetrated by a few bad actors. Republicans may find the "bad apples" view appealing because it absolves their leaders of blame. (Assuming they don't blame Antifa and BLM, or the FBI and the CIA.) White progressives may also find it appealing, because it makes the insurrectionists seem fringe. Unfortunately, both views are badly mistaken. The insurrection was an eruption of subterranean forces that had been building for some time. Those forces have not disappeared. On the contrary, they are building again. A second eruption would likely be larger and more violent than the first. Large enough to bury American democracy for at least a generation.

The source of the growing pressure is a set of slow-moving changes in American society. The United States has slowly become less white; less Christian and less powerful; more diverse, secular, and cosmopolitan. And this collided with a certain conception of America as a white Christian nation favored by God and ruled by white Christian men ready to defend freedom and order with violence. The plume of symbols that was spewed up over the Capitol that day—racist, Christian, and nationalist—was a byproduct of these different forces. The defeat of the insurrection temporarily released some of the pressure. But it did not resolve the underlying question about what sort of nation America is to be.

Meanwhile, the political fault lines dividing America grow deeper. They now threaten to tear the country apart. Here, too, white Christian nationalism is working just beneath the surface. It is fast becoming the San Andreas Fault of American politics. Debates over racial injustice, policing, gun violence, economic policy, media polarization, COVID-19, voting rights, and democracy are just cracks on the surface of our politics. The deeper, existential debate over American identity underlies them all. There will be another eruption—and soon. Will this one be "the big one"? The one that finally topples the centuries-old structures of American democracy? The one that finally dissolves the Union?

In the preceding pages, we have looked at how white Christian nationalism shapes our present-day politics, and how it was formed by the politics of the past. We have mapped the landscape to understand its constitutive elements. We have drilled down through the various layers of white Christian nationalism that have built up over time. The final step in our "geological analysis" is risk assessment.

Here we're guided by three questions: Where is white Christian nationalism going? What might happen in a worst-case scenario? And what can Americans do to prevent that from happening?

America narrowly avoided "the big one" in 2020. But the threat remains. In fact, it is building up, day by day.


## WHERE IT'S GOING

It may seem contradictory to ask how a "conservative" movement is changing. Isn't the whole point of conservatism to prevent or slow change? This question rests on two misconceptions. The first is that contemporary white Christian nationalism is "conservative." It is not. It is "reactionary." It does not seek to preserve the status quo. Rather, it seeks to destroy the status quo and return to a mythical past: to "make America great again." The second misconception is that reactionary movements are themselves unchanging. They are not. As political theorist Corey Robin argues, such movements are only averse to *one* kind of change: change that threatens their power.[1] Where ideology and tactics are concerned, they are quite willing to change—even radically—in order to defend existing hierarchies or restore old ones. Indeed, they are even prepared to use violent and revolutionary means. This is why Trump's staunchest allies so often (mis)represent the spirit of 1690 as the spirit of 1776.

So, we should not be too surprised if white Christian nationalism has changed over time in order to defend and restore racial, rel, and political hierarchies. As we have seen, it has taken many different forms since it first emerged over three centuries ago. For the first few centuries, "white" meant English, then native-born whites; "Christian" meant Protestant. And "others" included anyone falling outside those overlapping categories. Following World War II, it evolved into "colorblind," "Judeo-Christian," "American exceptionalism." Whiteness became defined mainly in opposition to Blackness; Christianity was widened to include Catholics and Mormons and hyphenated to include (some) Jews, or at least so as not to seem anti-Semitic. And America became defined as a "global superpower" destined to oversee the "international order," which is to say, its own empire.

Today, white Christian nationalism is shifting its shape yet again.

Anti-Black animus is still a core element. But anti-immigrant nativism has grown in importance. Nativism as such is not new. It has a long history in the United States that roughly parallels periods of mass immigration—such as the last half century.[2] But it is important to remember that Ronald Reagan and George W. Bush were both pro-immigration. And so was the Republican establishment that backed them. No more. Republican politicians and pundits like Ted Cruz and Lou Dobbs first rose to national prominence for their harsh anti-immigrant stances. Border walls, Muslim bans, and winning trade wars were the signature issues of Donald Trump's 2016 campaign. Trump's campaign manager and his closest presidential advisers—Steve Bannon and Steven Miller—both embraced the "great replacement" conspiracy theory, the belief that left-wing elites were intentionally promoting non-white and non-Christian immigration with the goal of replacing white Christian voters and consolidating their power. Right-wing pundits have also seized on this narrative. In her 2015 book *Adios, America*, Ann Coulter explained, "The American electorate isn't moving to the left—it's shrinking. No minds have been changed. Democrats just brought in a new group of voters whose minds didn't need to be changed." Fox News host Tucker Carlson has mainstreamed this once fringe theory again as of mid-2021.[3]

The political strategy behind this shift is clear enough. America's demographics are changing. But rather than heed the advice of party leaders to become more "inclusive," the Republican Party decided to double down on white Christian nostalgia in order to mobilize its base and to appeal to nativism in order to expand its base. The nativist strategy of emphasizing birthplace over skin color allows Republicans to appeal to American-born Blacks and Hispanics. And that strategy was surprisingly successful. It proved highly effective in places like Texas and Florida. Donald Trump received more votes from Hispanic and Black men in these states in 2020 than in 2016.[4]

The boundaries of Christianity are also shifting again. They have expanded into territory once considered "secular." Until recently, most Americans would probably have defined being a Christian in terms of belonging and/or belief. Certainly, most social scientists did so. To be a Christian was to be a member of a church and/or to affirm certain beliefs (e.g., in God or the Bible). But today, calling oneself a "Christian" or even an "evangelical" is sometimes just a way of claiming membership in an ideological or political tribe or defending a certain "way of life." Rogers Brubaker has called this "civilizationist" religion.

We can follow the creeping secularization of the evangelical label in our data. We asked Americans to affirm whether they currently identify as "Christian" as well as to affirm whether they identify as a "born-again or evangelical Christian." Figure 4.1. shows the percent of those who identify with either group by their specific religious identification. We also include the religious breakdown of one of our key Christian nationalism measures—wanting the government to formally declare the United States a Christian nation. More than 15% of those who also identify as "Christian" also say they are secular or belong to another religion. What's more, nearly 19% of those who identify as "evangelical" also identify as "secular" or belong to a non-Christian religion. Notably, over one-fifth of those Americans who agree the United States should be declared a "Christian nation" are seculars or those of non-Christian faiths. Clearly, religious terms like "Christian" and "evangelical" are becoming markers of social identity and political views rather than just religious conviction.

We observe a similar blurring of boundaries at the level of ideas, where we find increasing overlap between religious "prophecy belief" and secular conspiracy theories. During and after the Trump presidency, for example, the End Times story became highly entangled with the so-called "QAnon" theory—the belief that a secret cabal of Satan-worshiping liberal elites was trafficking, sexually abusing, and cannibalizing young children.[5] In a poll conducted in October 2020, political scientist Paul Djupe found 73% of

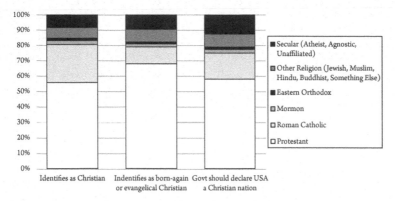

Figure 4.1. Percentage of Americans by specific religious tradition across indicators of Christian identity and Christian nationalism.

**Source:** *Public Discourse and Ethics Survey (Wave 1: August 2019; Wave 7: February 2021)*

Americans who scored in the top 25% of our Christian nationalism scale also affirmed core tenets of the QAnon conspiracy.

At the level of movements, evolving Christian definitions have also led to a greater overlap and interaction between the religious right and white nationalists. This is not new of course. The old religious right overlapped with the Ku Klux Klan, for instance.[6] But the old Republican establishment would not have accepted support from militia groups. Whatever you may think of his policies, it is difficult to imagine George H.W. Bush calling the Charlottesville marchers "very fine people."

The meaning of "America" and "patriotism" are also mutating from internationalism to isolationism. Or rather reverting. Because, like nativism, isolationism is nothing new. It is at least as old as George Washington's well-known warning about the dangers of "entangling alliances." During the early 20th century though, conservative Republicans were often isolationists, and Democrats were the internationalists. But this changed during the Cold War. Democrats were chastened by the debacle in Vietnam and became increasingly antiwar. And Republican "neoconservatives" and "hawks" proudly touted the United States as "the necessary nation" and the "global hegemon."

Importantly, religious and social conservatives who had once been vocal isolationists now joined the internationalist chorus. Their motivations were partly theological. They understood the Cold War as a fight against "godless communism." They viewed the "War on Terror" as a battle against an "Axis of Evil." But they were also motivated by their commitment to overseas missionary work. The security umbrella of the "Pax Americana" made it possible for American evangelicals to travel freely and spread their version of the Gospel throughout the world. Evangelical leaders such as Billy Graham blurred the lines between American imperialism and American Christianity with their language of "missions" and "crusades."[7]

No longer. The "neocon" hawks have become #NeverTrumpers and the isolationist fringe has become the Republican mainstream.[8] The new mantra is "strong borders," the new external enemy is China. Not so much "godless communist" China as much as "eating our lunch" capitalist China.

The stakes of today's cold war appear to be economic. But they do have an ideological aspect, insofar as they call attention to an *internal* enemy: "globalists" (a term with long-standing, anti-Semitic undertones). As opposed to "nationalists," who are the "real Americans." Donald Trump set the tone. After proudly calling himself a "nationalist" at a rally in 2018, he juxtaposed his nationalism with globalist democratic candidates, explaining, "You know what a globalist is, right? A globalist is a person who wants the globe to do well, frankly not caring about our country so much. And, you know what? We can't have that."[9]

Partisan trends are mirrored by religious and social conservatives who have happily joined into the new isolationist chorus. Thought leaders in these camps have even invented a theological rationale for the new nationalism that sounds eerily similar to the racial separatism arguments of decades past. God divided humanity into nations, they patiently explain. As theologians and pastors from Wayne Grudem to Robert Jeffress have repeatedly said, Jerusalem had walls, Heaven will have walls, border walls are God's idea. What's more, God enjoins Christians to obey—and enforce—the laws. That includes immigration laws. Especially immigration laws, in fact. In other words: God wants you to stay in the nation where he put you.[10]

Thus far, the new vocabulary of Christian nationalism includes three entries: nativism, civilizationism, and isolationism. But we need to add at least two more words to complete this updated dictionary: "grievance" and "messianism."

Much has been said about the importance of "grievance politics" and about the way in which a loss of status has contributed to feelings of persecution among conservative white Christians. But it is still worth underlining just how new this is. Traditionally, the deep story was recounted in a triumphalist tone. For nearly four centuries, many white American Christians had imagined themselves as racially, politically, and religiously superior to their opponents du jour. Today, they imagine themselves playing defense rather than offense. "Fighting" has replaced "winning." And the opposition is getting stronger. Or so they fear.

We can document this growing fear with recent data. In February 2021 we asked Americans how much discrimination they thought whites and Christians experienced now and how much discrimination they thought either group would experience within the next year. Figure 4.2 shows the predicted percentage

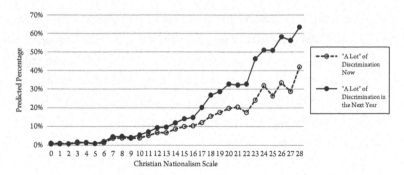

Figure 4.2. Predicted percentage of whites who believe both whites and Christians experience "A Lot" of Discrimination now and will experience discrimination within the next year across Christian nationalism.

**Notes:** Binary logistic regression models including Christian nationalism scale, age, gender, education, income, region, religious tradition, religious commitment, political party identification, and political conservatism.

**Source:** *Public Discourse and Ethics Survey (Wave 7; February 2021)*

of white Americans who said both whites and Christians experience "A Lot" of discrimination today and who said whites and Christians would experience "A Lot" of discrimination in the next year. Clearly, as Christian nationalism increases, white Americans are more likely to feel whites and Christians were discriminated against in early 2021. Notice, too, that the percentage goes up considerably when we asked whites about the discrimination they anticipated starting just after Biden's inauguration. Evidently, white Christian nationalists fear that persecution will increase under a Democrat—to the point where nearly two-thirds of those at the extreme end anticipate "A Lot" of discrimination for *both* whites and Christians.

The fifth and final change that is important to note is the sudden march toward messianism. Social scientists have repeatedly debunked the claim that religious conservatives had to "hold their noses" when they voted for Trump. A few may have. But most loved him; they loved him early; and that love has only grown over time. They loved him not only because they trusted him, but because they saw him as a savior and protector who would defend them from their enemies.[11] As we see above in Figure 4.2, the Christian nationalist hope in Trump as a "savior" is just as much about what Trump promised to save white conservative Christians *from*, namely, being marginalized and persecuted.

We asked Americans in October 2020, just before the election, how much discrimination whites and Christians experienced at that time, and how much discrimination they thought these groups would experience if either Trump or Biden were to win in November. Figure 4.3 plots the percentage of white Americans who thought both whites and Christians experienced "A Lot" of discrimination now and the percentage who thought these groups would experience "A Lot" of discrimination if either candidate were to

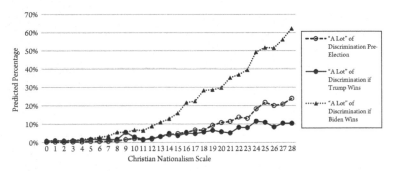

Figure 4.3. Predicted percentage of whites who believed both whites and Christians experience "A Lot" of discrimination in October 2020, if Trump won, or if Biden won the election across Christian nationalism.

**Notes:** Binary logistic regression models with Christian nationalism scale, age, gender, education, income, region, religious tradition, religious commitment, political party identification, and political conservatism.

**Source:** *Public Discourse and Ethics Survey (Wave 5; October 2020)*

win across our Christian nationalism scale. Even at high levels of Christian nationalism, the percentage of whites who felt whites and Christians would experience "A Lot" of discrimination if Trump won stays relatively low, well below the percentage who felt these groups were experiencing much discrimination before the election. A second term for Trump, in other words, meant these groups would be more protected. But look at how the threat of a Biden presidency skyrockets across scores on the Christian nationalism scale. Among whites who affirm Christian nationalist ideology the most, well over half felt *both* whites and Christians would experience "A Lot" of discrimination under Biden. From their perspective, Trump would not only redeem America from its downward slide like he promised in 2016, he would rescue whites and Christians from extreme victimization.

Trump once described himself as "the chosen one," albeit in a somewhat joking tone.[12] But some of his Christian supporters didn't seem to be in on the joke, perhaps because the joke was on them. A few even call him "the anointed one," a biblical term once reserved for the Israelite kings.[13] In religious versions of the QAnon theory, moreover, Trump is often cast in the role of an avenging Christ, who would punish the pederasts on a day of judgment known as "the Storm."[14] Of course, American history is full of charismatic preachers. But not of infallible political messiahs. That, too, is something new.

Should this messiah return—as a democratically elected candidate, leader of another bloody coup attempt, or victor in a Putin-style sham election—what would his kingdom look like? What would he and his supporters do to "make America great again"? Would this spell the end of American democracy?

## THE LOOMING THREAT

Throughout this book, we have argued that white Christian nationalism is becoming a serious threat to American democracy. Now it is time to make clear what we mean by "democracy" and why white Christian nationalism is in fact a threat, perhaps even a mortal one.

By "democracy," we mean what political philosophers call "liberal democracy." Democracy simply means rule by "the people." Liberal democracy has a number of additional features. These include universal suffrage, human rights, and equality under the law, among others.[15]

The first and most fundamental way in which white Christian nationalism threatens American liberal democracy is that it defines "the people" in a way that excludes many Americans. White Christian nationalism is a form of what is often called "ethno-nationalism."[16] It defines national belonging in terms of race, religion, and native birth. Liberal democracy rests on what is usually called "civic nationalism." It defines the nation in terms of values, laws, and institutions.

Echoing the first lines of the Constitution, and decades of conservative rhetoric, Trump supporters often spoke of themselves as "we, the people," as if their political opponents were not, and could not be "real Americans." This is one reason why so many were quick to embrace Trump's "Big Lie" about the "stolen election." If the "real" people had voted, then wouldn't Trump have won? If he lost, then there has to have been fraud. Maybe "foreigners" interfered. Perhaps "illegal immigrants" were voting. Or perhaps China had smuggled in fake ballots. Following up on this theory, one pro-Trump group even examined ballots cast in Arizona for traces of bamboo.[17]

Because it reinforces a narrow, ethno-nationalist definition of "the people," white Christian nationalism primes its followers to demand "election integrity" reforms that restrict ballot access for their opponents. Especially when they lose. Right before the 2020 election, white Christian nationalism was strongly correlated with the view that it is "too easy to vote." Right after the election, that correlation became even stronger (See Figure 4.4). Even after accounting for partisanship and political ideology, the more strongly white Americans affirm Christian nationalism, the more likely they were to respond to Trump's election loss with a view that voting access should be restricted even more.

Of course, voter suppression is as American as apple pie.[18] The Jim Crow system was premised on it. So was Republican electoral strategy. As we mentioned, Republican strategist Paul Weyrich said, "I don't want everybody to vote," long before Donald Trump was on the scene. Four decades later, in April of 2021, a spokesperson

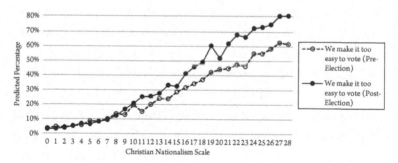

Figure 4.4. Predicted percentage of whites who believe we make it too easy to vote in October (pre-election) and November (post-election) across Christian nationalism.

**Notes:** Binary logistic regression models including Christian nationalism scale, age, gender, education, income, region, religious tradition, religious commitment, political party identification, and political conservatism.

**Source:** *Public Discourse and Ethics Survey (Wave 5: October 2020; Wave 6: November 2020)*

for Heritage Action, a conservative lobbying group that Weyrich founded, boasted about her organization's role in drafting voter suppression laws for Republican-controlled legislatures.[19]

One thing has changed since 2020 though: what was once done quietly behind closed doors is now being done loudly in the public square. According to the Brennan Center for Justice, as of late Spring 2021, nearly 400 voter suppression laws had been introduced, most prominently in Texas and Georgia, both historically Republican but now heavily contested. Nearly all such laws are transparently aimed at restricting voter access through stringent ID requirements, reducing early voting, purging voter rolls, and so on. Not since the Jim Crow era has voter suppression been undertaken so openly.

Voting rights are not the only rights that white Christian nationalism undermines. In fact, it leads to a philosophy of unequal rights: "rights for me, but not for thee." We already observed this philosophy in action when we contrasted reactions of white Christian nationalists to Black Lives Matter and the Capitol insurrection during 2020 and 2021. But it was also in evidence the following year, when conservative pundits and politicians decried left-wing "cancel culture" and "political correctness," even as they themselves "canceled" Rep. Liz Cheney for calling out the "Big Lie" and passed laws banning "Critical Race Theory" from public schools and universities. The state of Texas later passed legislation "canceling" Martin Luther King, Jr., by voting to remove his "I have a dream" speech from its civics curriculum.[20]

Nor are such impulses limited to the Republican base. Illiberal and antidemocratic currents have grown steadily more powerful among conservative Christian intellectuals since Trump took office. In some Catholic circles, critiques of philosophical and theological liberalism have become almost de rigueur. Patrick Deneen of Notre

Dame has decried "the failure of liberalism," holding it responsible for all manner of modern, social ills. Columnist and editor Sohrab Ahmari goes further, arguing that conservatives must "impose our order and our orthodoxy" on the rest of the nation, in order to secure "the highest good."[21] Likewise, Adrian Vermeule of the Harvard Law School has sought to revive Catholic "integralism," the view that the state should be subject to the authority of the church, as it was in Spain under the Franco dictatorship.[22] Nor are such views confined to the Catholic right. The former editor of the conservative *National Review*, Rich Lowry, has recently argued explicitly for the return of "cultural nationalism" and a rejection of multiculturalism.[23] Meanwhile, the Calvinist conservative Peter Leithart has recently extolled the virtues of Constantine, the Roman emperor who declared Christianity the official religion of Rome and hunted down "pagans."[24] Of course, Christian Reconstructionists have been advocating a return to theocracy for over half a century now.[25] And though relatively few Americans would even be able to define "integralism" or "reconstructionism," let alone pledge their allegiance to these movements, their core elements pervade mainstream Christian nationalism.

The growing chorus of authoritarian sentiment among conservative Christian intellectuals is not just empty chatter. It is a leading indicator of a broader shift on the religious right. So long as natural-born white Christians were the dominant group, numerically and culturally, they did not need to directly challenge America's democratic institutions. Confronted with minority status and diminishing power, some are now prepared to reject liberal democracy in favor of "stronger measures." Two prominent conservatives, one a former Trump official, even mused on air about "lessons learned" from the Capitol insurrection and the possible advantages of an American monarchy.[26] What would happen if such people got their way? To answer this question, one need only look at other illiberal regimes that have already undermined liberal democracy.

## WHAT MIGHT HAPPEN

There is nothing exceptional about the growth of illiberalism in America. Christian nationalists have allied with right-wing populists in many other countries, too.[27] Hungary, Poland, Russia, and the Philippines have been ruled by such an alliance for some time now. Brazil recently joined their ranks, too. Nor are all religious nationalists *Christian* nationalists. Similar alliances have also taken power in Turkey (Sunni Muslim), India (Hindu), and Myanmar (Buddhism) as well.[28]

As Harvard political scientists Steven Levitsky and Daniel Ziblatt outline in their influential book *How Democracies Die*, the recent history of these regimes provides some worrisome clues about how a second Trump presidency might unfold.[29] Like Trump, the leaders of these regimes all came into power via democratic elections. Once in power, however, they instituted changes that made it difficult—*very* difficult—to remove them from office again.

American institutions already provide several mechanisms that a minority party can exploit to retain power. The first is the Electoral College, which makes it possible to win the presidency without winning the popular vote, as happened in 2000 and again in 2016. The second is partisan gerrymandering, which allows politicians to choose their voters, rather than the other way around. Both, by virtue of their overrepresentation in rural areas, greatly magnify the power of the Republican Party and conservative voters.[30] As a result, the number of seats that the GOP controls in state legislatures is often highly disproportionate to their share of the popular vote.

The same is true of many states' congressional delegations as well. In 2020, for example, the GOP won less than 49% of the popular vote in Pennsylvania, but more than 56% of the seats in the state legislature.

Not surprisingly, support for the Electoral College and partisan gerrymandering is highly correlated with support for Christian nationalism (See Figure 4.5). Even after holding factors like partisanship or political ideology constant, Christian nationalism is powerfully associated with whites being unwilling to address gerrymandering or support electing the president by popular vote. Instead, white Christian nationalism clearly favors the Electoral College system. These findings suggest that the "populism" linked with white Christian nationalism is an *authoritarian* populism, one that happily exchanges democratic procedure for tribal victory.

Outside of the United States, authoritarian populist leaders rarely do away with elections entirely. But they often change election

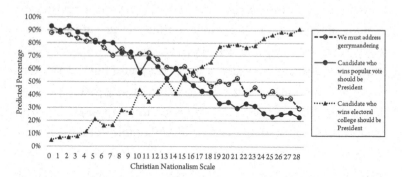

Figure 4.5. Predicted percentage of whites who agree with addressing gerrymandering, support the popular vote, or support the electoral college across Christian nationalism.

**Notes:** Binary logistic regression models including Christian nationalism scale, age, gender, education, income, region, religious tradition, religious commitment, political party identification, and political conservatism.

**Source:** *Public Discourse and Ethics Survey (Wave 5; October 2020)*

rules to their advantage: rules governing who can vote, how votes are counted, how those votes translate into seats, how electoral districts are drawn, how parliamentary alliances are formed, and so on. And when these changes failed to deliver the expected result, the leaders sometimes nullified the results and called new elections.

Having changed the rules, autocrats then change the umpires: the courts. By appointing loyalist judges, populist strongmen prevent legal challenges to the new election laws and to other "reforms" that favored them and their allies. (In this vein, the new conservative supermajority on the US Supreme Court eviscerated what remained of the Voting Rights Act in July of 2021 in *Brnovich v. Democratic National Committee*). And when that failed to yield the desired result, they sometimes expanded the courts, changed their jurisdictions, or simply dissolved them altogether. And when the courts nonetheless issued rulings not to their liking, they simply ignored them.

Having "reformed" the electoral and judicial systems, they then focused their attention on the legislatures. Or, rather, on transferring as many of their powers as possible to the chief executive, which is to say, themselves. Sometimes, states of emergency were declared. Sometimes, executive decrees were released. But everywhere, power was centralized. Liberal democracy slowly gave way to authoritarian rule in a strongman regime. Trump made no secret of his admiration for authoritarian rulers like Vladimir Putin. Or, rather, his admiration for their dictatorial power. And many of his followers shared his esteem for Russia, which they imagined (incorrectly) as a white Christian nation. (In this vein, after Trump's defeat in 2020, Republican-controlled state governments in Georgia and elsewhere centralized election administration in their own hands in the name of "election integrity" and "voting reform.")

Meanwhile, corruption took root. Not just as a strategy of self-enrichment; but also as a strategy of political control. Political power was used to accumulate economic resources. But also the reverse. The leader, his family, and their inner circles used state power to enrich themselves. They took control of mineral resources. They steered state contracts to friends. They siphoned public funds into offshore accounts. They kept some of this wealth for their personal use. And they also "invested" some of it in their powerful supporters who in turn "reinvested" some of it in their own supporters building vast patronage networks that stretched from corrupt billionaires on top to small-time hacks on the bottom. Those who refused to play the game and tried to build up rival networks were harassed, expropriated, or even exterminated. Trump, himself, took steps in this direction during his time in office.

Sometimes the violence was carried out by law enforcement, intelligence officials, or the uniformed military. At other times it was carried out by vigilante groups and paramilitary organizations who shared the regime's ideology. Or by criminal gangs who just wanted to share in its spoils.

The targets of these attacks were not just political or economic rivals, however. Strongman regimes also seek to control culture.[31] Thus, journalists, academics, and religious leaders were often subject to intimidation, imprisonment, or execution. At the same time, every effort was made to coerce and cajole the media, the universities, and the religious communities to toe the line and support the regime. Opposition newspapers, dissident faculties, and rebellious houses of worship were closed. Pro-regime organizations were erected in their place.

But the harshest violence is often reserved for "internal enemies" of the regime, however defined: Muslims in India, Rohingya in

Myanmar, or Roma in Hungary. Even in Brazil, the rise of charismatic evangelicalism in concert with a populist authoritarian regime has led to a persecution of traditional Afro-Brazilian religions. In each situation, targets are subjected to mob violence, ethnic cleansing, and extrajudicial killing.

None of this happened overnight of course. Democracies don't die suddenly with the bang of a gun; instead, they are slowly suffocated with a knee to the neck. Given the trends we've documented, is American liberal democracy going to suffer the same fate?

## COULD IT HAPPEN HERE?

The Capitol insurrection may well prove to have been a test run for 2024. In 2020, Trump's efforts to overturn the election and remain in the White House only failed because enough Republican officials in local and state offices refused to go along with it, and because enough Republican-appointed judges dismissed his campaign's various legal appeals. Make no mistake: this will not happen again. Trump and his allies have learned their lesson. Those who opposed the insurrection or challenged the "Big Lie" are in the process of being replaced by a partisan loyalist or stripped of their power. Just ask Liz Cheney or Brad Raffensperger. And given how closely contested American elections are these days, rigging or changing the outcome in just a few purple states would be enough for Trump or a Trump loyalist to lay claim to the White House. This is perhaps the more likely road back to power.

The only real question is whether the next Republican revolt will succeed. The answer to that question will not be determined solely at the ballot box. Rather, it will also be decided through a wide-ranging, behind-the-scenes political struggle involving various power centers. The outcome of the struggle is hard to foresee, though it will likely involve episodes of violence. But the distribution of various types of power does provide us with some important clues about how it might unfold. A Trumpist victory that would end democracy is a real possibility, but it is by no means a foregone conclusion, and for two reasons: the dispersion of power and the diversity of the country.

Political power is more decentralized in the United States than in most countries, including many of those where illiberal regimes have taken control. In part, this is a function of America's constitutional design. Having grown up in the shadow of monarchy, and studied the history of tyranny, the founders had a healthy fear of centralized rule, and sought to forestall it by dispersing governmental power. They granted sovereignty to the individual states, but also to the federal government. They separated the powers of government into three independent branches, and the state governments followed their lead. They also disbanded the Revolutionary Army, and opposed standing armies, because they knew that many tyrants had begun their careers as military officers. They opposed the creation of a National Bank for similar reasons: they knew that large concentrations of private wealth often lead to oligarchic rule.

Nor is America's constitutional design the only obstacle to centralized rule by a strongman. In many countries, economic, political and cultural power are all concentrated in just one city (e.g., London, Paris, and Tokyo). To take control of the country, one only needs to take control of the capital city. Not so in the United States. There, the territorial expansion of the United States led to a further decentralization of power. Not just the political power of large states such as New York, Florida, Texas, and California. But also economic power. Movies are made in Los Angeles, apps are coded in Silicon

Valley, oil is traded in Houston, bonds are auctioned in New York, and military spending is determined in Washington, to name just a few salient examples. Seizing control of all of these power centers would not be easy.

Cultural power is also widely dispersed in the United States. Importantly, America's leading universities are not under federal control; neither are its radio and television stations. And they are being rapidly replaced by social media outlets, which are also in private hands. This makes it more difficult to suppress dissent and control "messaging" in the way that populist strongmen do in other countries. Just imagine if Donald Trump had had the power to replace the entire faculty of the University of California system, shut down CNN, and ban people from Twitter. Does anyone seriously think he would have hesitated to do so?

The same is true of America's religious communities. Religious freedom has created multiple and competing religious bodies with divergent views on politics. In sum, there is just not one elite in America, nor just one key city or community, but many of all three. And these elites, cities, and communities have conflicting interests and ideologies. All of which creates another formidable obstacle to the aspiring demagogue. James Madison would be pleased.

Cultural power is "soft power." What about the "hard power" of state violence? Here, too, the dispersion of power creates an obstacle to full-blown tyranny. In many countries, there is one police force under central control. In the United States, there are countless police forces under state and local control. To be sure, this often allows local police forces to evade federal oversight. And sometimes even to collude with local vigilantes, as in the Jim Crow era. But it also shields them from a centralized takeover by a would-be tyrant. Imagine if the police forces in Baltimore, Ferguson, and

Portland had all been under federal control during the Trump presidency?

Nor is this the only such obstacle nor perhaps even the most important. In many countries, members of the police and the military are drawn from the dominant racial or religious group. Subordinate groups are effectively excluded. Not so in the United States. Long-standing efforts to integrate America's armed forces have been quite successful. Similar efforts to integrate local law enforcement have been somewhat spottier, but not entirely unsuccessful, particularly in the major cities. Why is this important? Because multiracial and multicultural corps of military and law enforcement offices are much less likely to support the kind of avowedly or tacitly racist and Christianist regime that Trump and his white Christian nationalist supporters dream about.

In sum, the dispersion of political, economic, cultural, and military power across multiple institutions, regions, and elites, and the growing diversity of these same elites, would make it quite difficult for an ambitious strongman to achieve a high degree of centralized control. Much as Trump might like to emulate Putin, Erdoğan, or Kim, it is unlikely that he would be able to do so.

## JIM CROW 2.0

The more probable outcome, should Trump and his allies return to power, is what the South African sociologist Pierre Van Den Bergh calls *Herrenvolk* democracy, which he defines as "a parliamentary regime in which the exercise of power and suffrage is restricted, *de facto* and often *de jure*, to the dominant group," which understands itself as a superior race or culture, and in which other races and subcultures are subjected to varying degrees of legal discrimination and violent subjugation.[32] Let's call it Jim Crow 2.0.

Like the original Jim Crow, it would be regionally concentrated in MAGA states. There, subordinate groups and political dissidents would be subjected to various forms of legal discrimination, public humiliation, and vigilante violence. The harshest treatment would likely be reserved for non-white, undocumented immigrants, who might be subjected to mass deportations on an unprecedented scale. In Jim Crow 2.0, Brown could become the new Black.

Such a regime would be widely resisted in anti-MAGA states, of course, and effectively so. The MAGA regime would certainly try to use the powers of the federal government and judiciary to force the "blue states" into line. It might deny federal money to "sanctuary cities" that refused to cooperate with its policies of mass deportation, for example, or it might deny research dollars to universities that continued to mandate diversity training or teach critical race theory, the right's latest bugaboo. But the deep blue states of the West Coast and the Northeast would have enough power and resources to resist such attempts at coercion.

If the MAGA regime endured for two decades or more—and most authoritarian regimes do—existing trends toward self-sorting along ideological lines would likely continue or even accelerate. MAGA-minded whites might follow libertarian-leaning "tech bros" and "finance bros" from California and New York to Texas and Florida. College-educated white professionals might migrate in the other direction, leaving suburban Dallas and Orlando for suburban Chicago and Seattle. At this point in the process, argues Never Trump conservative David French, secession scenarios and even civil war would start to become live possibilities.[33] The result could be the dissolution of the Union.

Like the original Jim Crow, *Herrenvolk* democracy would only ever really be finally dislodged via a prolonged and costly campaign of civil disobedience, mass protest, and economic boycotts that significantly disrupted life in the MAGA states. Like the first and second civil rights movements, it could last several decades and might require multiple attempts. The odds are that a second Trump presidency would evolve into a longer-lived Trump Dynasty, with power eventually passing to one of Trump's children.

Trumpist America would not be Hitler's Germany. But it would not be so far removed from Putin's Russia either. And like this and other populist and kleptocratic regimes, it would be characterized by governmental incompetence accompanied by gradual economic decline. Ironically, a serious attempt to "make America great again" would probably end up making it chaotic and poor.

## WHAT CAN BE DONE?

America is at a crossroads. It has been there before. More than once. To the left lies a path toward a multiracial democracy; to the right lies a path toward continued white dominance. In the past, America has sometimes turned left for a time, only to veer sharply back to the right. This is what happened in 1787 when it incorporated slavery into the Constitution, in 1877 when it turned the South over to Confederate "Redeemers," and in 1968 when it chose "law and order" over civil rights.[34] Each time, the country took two steps forward, then one step back.

Which way will it turn this time? Now, as in the past, the answer will depend in part on which path white Christians choose. But it will also depend on whether secular progressives are willing to ally with people of faith who share their commitment to liberal democracy.

What is needed now is a popular front stretching from democratic socialists such as Alexandria Ocasio-Cortez and Bernie Sanders not only to classical liberals such as Bill Kristol and David French but also to cosmopolitan #NeverTrump evangelicals like Russell Moore, Beth Moore, or Tim Keller. The ideological distance that separates the end points of this alliance is considerable. There are deep disagreements about policy issues such as abortion and inequality. But also an overarching consensus about liberal democratic principles such as voting rights, racial justice, freedom of religion, and the rule of law.

In deciding which way to turn, conservative white Christians might start by confronting their own history. Like any history, it is morally complex. There is plenty to be ashamed of. White Protestant theology has provided theological justifications for racism, imperialism, and exploitation. In some cases, it still does. This is not just a matter of "racial prejudice" or "personal morality." Instead, it has to do with the deep story that shapes many Christians' perceptions of the present in ways that they may not even be consciously aware of. Reckoning with white Christian nationalism means more than "looking into one's heart"; it also means reckoning with your tribe's history. It means confronting, not just your own sins, but also "the sins of the fathers."

Of course, there is also much that contemporary evangelicals can be proud of. There have always been some white Christians who saw racism, imperialism, and exploitation as the sins that they were and are. And who struggled for another America, based on equality, inclusion, and the common good. There still are. We have met many of them in these pages. While some parts of the evangelical past are regrettable, others are laudable. In charting a path toward a multiracial and multicultural America, white conservative Christians might look back to figures such as Roger Williams or William Penn, for

whom Christian faith went hand in hand with civility and toleration. There is no shortage of resources in American Christianity that
might help chart the way forward.

Building a popular front in defense of liberal democracy will also
require that secular progressives confront their past as well. Secular
progressivism is the offspring of liberal Protestantism.[35] It, too, has
a history that is morally complex, because it, too, is entwined with
white Christian nationalism, specifically, with the WASP imperialist version of the early 20th century. Secular progressivism also has
its deep story. In that story, a morally and intellectually advanced
elite shepherds a backward and benighted mass toward prosperity
and enlightenment.[36] In the early 20th century, this deep story
was entangled with nativism, imperialism, and eugenics. Today, it
is tinged with "workism," meritocracy, and technocracy.[37] And, in
many cases, with an instinctive antipathy toward organized religion,
which is regarded as a mortal threat to personal autonomy or even
as a form of "child abuse." If they are really serious about liberal democracy, then secular progressives will also have to set aside some
of their own most deeply held prejudices, prejudices that have also
played an important role in stoking populist resentment and driving
political polarization.

America is an experiment. It is an attempt to build a nation of
nations and a people of peoples; and also to build a representative democracy on a continental scale. It is not inevitable or even
clear that the experiment will succeed. The challenge is twofold: to
maintain social solidarity amid deep diversity; and to sustain civic
engagement in a mass democracy. Neither is easy. In the past, democratic republics were usually small in scale and homogeneous in culture. Indeed, some political philosophers believed that Republican
government was *only* possible in such contexts. For more than two

centuries, the United States has defied their predictions. Whether there will be another American century, and whether that century will be democratic, remains to be seen. Much will depend upon the decisions that individual Americans make in the next few years, and also on the alliances that they forge.

Donald Trump and his most zealous followers have already made their decision: they have rejected America's experiment in multiracial democracy in favor of white Christian nationalism.

Whether they are successful is up to the rest of us.

# ACKNOWLEDGMENTS

The brevity of this volume belies the enormous number of colleagues, institutions, and friends who have influenced its writing. We would gratefully single out each one of the names listed below and recount the interactions and support that have spurred us on, but then the acknowledgments would be longer than the book.

In alphabetical order, we express our sincerest appreciation for Sinem Adar, Einstein Fellows, Berlin; Carol and John Albright; Scott Appleby and Atalia Omer, "Contending Modernities," Notre Dame; Joseph O. Baker; Loretta Bass; Rita Hermon-Belot, École des hautes études en sciences sociales; Michelle Boorstein, *The Washington Post*; Ruth Braunstein; Annika Brockschmidt; Delf Bucher, *Reformiert*; Anthea Butler; Clemens Carl and Beatrix Dombrowski, Herder Verlag; John Carlson, Center for the Study of Religion and Conflict, University of Arizona; Shaun Casey, Berkley Center for Religion, Peace, and World Affairs at Georgetown; Jocelyn Cesari; Jerome Copulsky; Caroline Mala Corbin; Tobias Cremer; Joshua T. Davis; Angela Denker; Toby Dodge, Social Science Research Council; Paul Djupe; Kristin Kobes Du Mez; Penny

Edgell, MOSAIC, University of Minnesota; Thomas Edsall, *New York Times*; John Fea, "Current Pub"; François Foret, CEVIPOL, Free University of Brussels; Kenneth Frantz; Tom Gjelten, NPR; Eliza Griswold, *The New Yorker*; Jeff Guhin; Conrad Hackett and Greg Smith, Pew Research Center; Sam Haselby; Patrick Hough and Peter Wicks, Elm Institute; James Davison Hunter, Charles Mathewes, and Isaac Ariail Reed, Institute for Advanced Studies in Culture, University of Virginia; Julie Ingersoll; Adrien Jaulmes, *Le Figaro*; Hans Joas, Marcia Pally, Rolf Schieder, Department of Theology, Humboldt University, Berlin; Jack Jenkins; Robert P. Jones, PRRI; Robert Kehoe, *The Point Magazine*; Matthias Koenig; Andreas Lesch, *Bistumspresse*; Michael Luo, *The New Yorker*; Gerardo Marti; Colin McEnroe, WNPR; Paul D. Miller; Peter Manseau; Yascha Mounk, "The Good Fight" podcast; Anne Nelson; Bradley Onishi, "Straight White American Jesus"; Diane Orson NPR/CT Public Radio; Willimien Otten and William Schultz, Rustandy Center, University of Chicago; Sarah Posner; Princeton Center for Human Values; Hartmut Rosa, University of Jena; Andrew Seidel, Freedom from Religion Foundation; Ayelet Shachar and Steven Vertovec, Max Planck Institute for the Study of Religious and Ethnic Diversity, Göttingen; Jyotirmaya Sharma; Landon Schnabel; Mark Silk, Religion News Service; Jason Stanley; Frauke Steffens, *Frankfurter Allgemeine Zeitung*; Dante Stewart; Katherine Stewart; Chrissy Stroop; Mathis Trapp, *WDR*, Katja Ridderbusch, *Deutschlandfunk*, Christiane Florin,"Tag für Tag, *Deutschlandradio*; Reinhard Bingener, *Frankfurter Allgemeine Zeitung*; Friederike Schulte, Carl-Schurz-Haus, Freiburg; Jay Tolson, *The Hedgehog Review*; Amanda Tyler, BJC; Pierre-Antoine Ullmo, "EXP Expeditions"; Marietta van der Tol, Landecker Seminar, Blavatnik School, Oxford; Miroslav Volf; Jon Ward, "The Long Game" podcast; Andrew Whitehead; Daniel Wildman, Leo Baeck Institute,

London; Jonathan Wilson-Hartgrove; Monika Wohlrab-Sahr and Marian Burchardt, "Multiple Secularities" Research Group, Leipzig; Geneviève Zubrzycki.

We must single out a few names for special thanks.

We are so grateful to Jemar Tisby for writing the Foreword. His work has been a tremendous influence on our own, and his enthusiastic support means more to us than we can express in so few words.

Thanks go to Martin van Gelderen and the Lichtenberg Kolleg and Moritz Stern Institut, Göttingen. They provided generous support for Philip Gorski's sabbatical year, during which he developed numerous ideas and arguments contained in this volume.

The Public Discourse and Ethics Survey would have never been possible without the work of Joshua B. Grubbs and generous support from the Charles C. Koch Foundation. Dr. Grubbs not only procured the funding, but arranged the data collection through YouGov, and graciously allowed Samuel Perry to include numerous questions on the survey instrument. The benefit of access to those data for understanding Christian nationalism in the United States has been incalculable.

We're also grateful to Theo Calderara and the whole team at Oxford University Press for their vision for this book and tireless work along the way.

Lastly, we also thank our families.

Phil: To my wife Hella and my sons Jacob, Eric, and Mark. Thanks for putting up with my endless thoughts about American politics.

Sam: To my wife Jill; my daughter Ryan; and my sons, Beau and Whitman. You fill my heart with endless motivation and joy.

# NOTES

*Introduction*

1. Bradley Onishi, "Trump's New Civil Religion," *New York Times*, January 19, 2021, Opinion.
2. Thomas B Edsall, "'The Capitol Insurrection Was as Christian Nationalist as It Gets," *The New York Times*, January 28, 2021.
3. Important treatments of Christian nationalism include Andrew Whitehead and Samuel Perry, *Taking America Back for God: Christian Nationalism in the United States* (New York: Oxford University Press, 2020); Michelle Goldberg, *Kingdom Coming: The Rise of Christian Nationalism*, 1st ed. (New York: W.W. Norton & Co., 2006). http://www.loc.gov/catdir/toc/ecip065/2005036593.html; Kevin M Kruse, *One Nation Under God: How Corporate America Invented Christian America* (New York: Basic Books, 2015); Philip Gorski, *American Babylon: Democracy and Christianity Before and After Trump* (London: Routledge, 2020); Katherine Stewart, *The Power Worshippers: Inside the Dangerous Rise of Religious Nationalism* (New York: Bloomsbury, 2019); Anthea Butler, *White Evangelical Racism: The Politics of Morality in America* (Chapel Hill: University of North Carolina Press Books, 2021).
4. Amy Sherman, "Post Wrongly Says Thousands of Ballots Sent to Dead People, Pets in Virginia and Nevada," *Politifact* (September 9, 2020). https://www.politifact.com/factchecks/2020/sep/09/facebook-posts/post-wrongly-says-thousands-ballots-sent-dead-peop/.
5. Robert P Jones, *The End of White Christian America* (New York: Simon and Schuster, 2016).

6. Jones, *The End of White Christian America*; Eric Kaufmann, *Whiteshift: Populism, Immigration and the Future of White Majorities* (Penguin UK, 2018); Timothy Snyder, *The Road to Unfreedom: Russia, Europe, America* (Tim Duggan Books, 2018). Jones, *The End of White Christian America*.

7. Arlie Russell Hochschild, *Strangers in Their Own Land: Anger and Mourning on the American right* (New York: The New Press, 2016); George Lakoff and Mark Johnson, *Metaphors We Live By* (Chicago: University of Chicago Press, 2008).

8. Joseph O Baker, Samuel L Perry, and Andrew L Whitehead, "Keep America Christian (and White): Christian Nationalism, Fear of Ethnoracial Outsiders, and Intention to Vote for Donald Trump in the 2020 Presidential Election," *Sociology of Religion* 81, no. 3 (2020); Bart Bonikowski, "Ethno-nationalist Populism and the Mobilization of Collective Resentment," *The British Journal of Sociology* 68 (2017); Diana C Mutz, "Status Threat, Not Economic Hardship, Explains the 2016 Presidential Vote," *Proceedings of the National Academy of Sciences* 115, no. 19 (2018).

9. On the myth of the Christian nation, see John Fea, *Was America Founded as a Christian Nation?*, Revised ed. (Louisville, KY: Westminster John Know Press, 2016); Andrew Seidel, *The Founding Myth: Why Christian Nationalism Is Un-American* (New York: Sterling, 2019); Steven K Green, *Inventing a Christian America: The Myth of a Religious Founding* (New York: Oxford University Press, 2015); Bernard Bailyn, *The Ideological Origins of the American Revolution*, Enl. ed. (Cambridge, MA: Belknap Press of Harvard University Press, 1992); Steven M Dworetz, *The Unvarnished Doctrine: Locke, Liberalism and the American Revolution* (Durham, NC: Duke University Press, 1989); Eric Nelson, *The Hebrew Republic: Jewish Sources and the Transformation of European Political Thought* (Cambridge, MA: Harvard University Press, 2011); Katherin Carté, *Religion and the American Revolution* (Chapel Hill: University of North Carolina Press, 2021); Sven Beckert and Seth Rockman, *Slavery's Capitalism: A New History of American Economic Development* (Philadelphia: University of Pennsylvania Press, 2016); Thomas M Shapiro, *Toxic Inequality: How America's Wealth Gap Destroys Mobility, Deepens the Racial Divide, and Threatens Our Future* (New York: Basic Books, 2017).

10. On the biblical sources of Christian nationalism, see Philip S Gorski, *American Covenant*, 2nd ed. (Princeton, NJ: Princeton University Press, 2019); Anthony D Smith, *Chosen Peoples: Sacred Sources of National Identity* (Oxford: Oxford University Press, 2004); Paul S Boyer, *When Time Shall Be No More: Prophecy Belief in Modern American Culture*, Studies in cultural history (Cambridge, MA: Harvard University Press, 1992); David Mark Whitford, *The Curse of Ham in the Early Modern Era: The Bible and the Justifications for Slavery* (London: Routledge, 2017); Gorski, *American Babylon: Democracy and Christianity Before and After Trump*.

11. Jemar Tisby, *The Color of Compromise: The Truth about the American Church's Complicity in Racism* (Grand Rapids, MI: Zondervan, 2019).

12. Robert Jewett and John Shelton Lawrence, *Captain America and the Crusade against Evil: The Dilemma of Zealous Nationalism* (Grand Rapids, MI: W.B. Eerdmans, 2003);Kaleigh Rogers, "Why QAnon Has Attracted So Many White Evangelicals," *FiveThirtyEight* (March 4, 2021).

13. Richard Slotkin, *Regeneration through Violence: The Mythology of the American Frontier, 1600–1860* (Norman, OK: University of Oklahoma Press, 2000); Richard Slotkin, *Gunfighter Nation: The Myth of the Frontier in Twentieth-Century America* (Norman: University of Oklahoma Press, 1998).

14. Jacob S Hacker and Paul Pierson, *Let Them Eat Tweets: How the Right Rules in an Age of Extreme Inequality* (New York: Liveright Publishing, 2020). See also Kaufman, *Whiteshift: Populism, Immigration and the Future of White Majorities*; Philip S Gorski, "The Long Withdrawing Roar. From Culture Wars to Culture Clashes," *The Hedgehog Review*, Summer 2021.

15. Jones, *The End of White Christian America*; Gorski, *American Babylon: Democracy and Christianity Before and After Trump*; Marisa Abrajano and Zoltan L Hajnal, *White Backlash* (Princeton, NJ: Princeton University Press, 2015); Carol Anderson, *One Person, No Vote: How Voter Suppression Is Destroying Our Democracy* (New York: Bloomsbury Publishing USA, 2018).

16. Emma Green, "White Evangelicals Believe They Face More Discrimination Than Muslims," *The Atlantic* (March 10, 2017).

17. Jill Lepore, *This America: The Case for the Nation* (Hachette, UK: Liveright 2019); Steven B Smith, *Reclaiming Patriotism in an Age of Extremes* (New Haven, CT: Yale University Press, 2021), pp. 23–24.

18. Steven Smith in his book on patriotism points out that Machiavelli and Rousseau both thought Christians couldn't be patriots because they were thinking about their eternal citizenship rather than the nation. Smith, *Reclaiming Patriotism in an Age of Extremes*.

19. https://twitter.com/albertmohler/status/727673203267670016?lang=en.

20. Ruth Igielnik, Scott Keeter, and Hannah Hartig, "Behind Biden's 2020 Victory: An Examination of the 2020 Electorate, Based on Validated Voters," *Pew Research Center* (June 30, 2021). https://www.pewresearch.org/politics/2021/06/30/behind-bidens-2020-victory/.

21. "Wheaton Faculty Have Released a Statement Condemning 'Abuses of Christian Symbols' at the Capitol," *Relevant*, January 12, 2021, https://www.relevantmagazine.com/current/nation/wheaton-college-capitol-raid/.Cheryl;K Chumley, *Socialists Don't Sleep: Christians Must Rise or America Will Fall* (New York: Humanix Books, 2020).

22. According to Pew's Religion and Politics Survey collected in January 2016 (available at www.thearda.com), white Americans who felt it was very important their candidate shared their religious beliefs, felt it was a bad thing that

religion was losing influence in the United States, and felt there was too little religious expression by political leaders were all more likely to favor Trump over Ben Carson, Ted Cruz, Marco Rubio, and Jeb Bush.

23.  Rogers Brubaker, "Between Nationalism and Civilizationism: The European Populist Moment in Comparative Perspective," *Ethnic and Racial Studies* 40, no. 8 (2017), pp 1191-1226. .

*Chapter 1*

1.  "A Reporter's Footage from Inside the Capitol Siege," *The New Yorker* (2021). https://www.newyorker.com/news/video-dept/a-reporters-footage-from-inside-the-capitol-siege?utm_medium=social&utm_brand=tny&mbid=soc ial_twitter&utm_source=twitter&utm_social-type=owned. See also "Inside the Capitol Riot: An Exclusive Video Investigation," *The New York Times* (2021). https://www.nytimes.com/2021/06/30/us/jan-6-capitol-attack-takeaways.html.

2.  Eric Kaufmann, *Whiteshift: Populism, Immigration and the Future of White Majorities.*

3.  We will only present our data in figures throughout the book. However, for details about the Public Discourse and Ethics Survey and regression tables corresponding to the figures, please refer to either author's department webpage.

4.  Andrew L Whitehead and Samuel L Perry, *Taking America Back for God: Christian Nationalism in the United States.*

5.  Paul A Djupe and Ryan P Burge, "What Is an Evangelical?," *Religion in Public* (May 7 2020). https://religioninpublic.blog/2020/05/07/what-is-an-evangelical/.

6.  One surprise: Jehovah's Witnesses score relatively high. This is unexpected considering the group was often criticized as "un-American" in the mid-20th century because it formally teaches that God's people should shun expressions of patriotism such as serving in the military or even saluting the flag. However, it is possible here that Jehovah's Witnesses are answering as extreme religious conservatives rather than with their formal theological teaching. This would also underscore an important point found elsewhere in our Christian nationalism research: our political theology is often determined more by our cultural and political tribe rather than the orthodox doctrines of our religious traditions.

7.  Hedieh Mirahmadi, "The Assault on 'White America,'" *The Christian Post* (April 8, 2021). https://www.christianpost.com/news/the-assault-on-white-america.html.

8. Joshua T Davis, "Funding God's Policies, Defending Whiteness: Christian Nationalism and Whites' Attitudes Towards Racially-Coded Government Spending," *Ethnic and Racial Studies* 42, no. 12 (2019); Ian Haney-López, *Dog Whistle Politics: How Coded Racial Appeals Have Reinvented Racism and Wrecked the Middle Class* (New York: Oxford University Press, 2015).

9. Samuel L Perry and Andrew L Whitehead, "Christian America in Black and White: Racial Identity, Religious-National Group Boundaries, and Explanations for Racial Inequality," *Sociology of Religion* 80, no. 3 (2019); Samuel L Perry, Andrew L Whitehead, and Joshua B Grubbs, "Prejudice and Pandemic in the Promised Land: How White Christian Nationalism Shapes Americans' Racist and Xenophobic Views of COVID-19," *Ethnic and Racial Studies* 44, no. 5 (2021).

10. James Baldwin, *The Fire Next Time* (New York: Vintage, 2013).

11. A small sampling of this genre of books by pastors and politicians affirming the creed of "American exceptionalism", a.k.a, Christian Nationalism: Newt Gingrich, *Rediscovering God in America* (Nashville, TN: Thomas Nelson, 2006); D James Kennedy, *What if America Were a Christian Nation Again?* (Nashville, TN: Thomas Nelson, 2003).

12. Jose F Figueroa, Rishi K Wadhera, Dennis Lee, Robert W Yeh, and Benjamin D Sommers. "Community-Level Factors Associated with Racial and Ethnic Disparities in COVID-19 Rates in Massachusetts," *Health Affairs* (2020). http://doi.org/10.1377/hlthaff.2020.01040. Chengzhen L Dai et al. 2021. "Characteristics and Factors Associated with Coronavirus Disease 2019 Infection, Hospitalization, and Mortality Across Race and Ethnicity," *Clinical Infectious Diseases* (2021). DOI: 10.1093/cid/ciab154.

13. Samuel L Perry, Andrew L Whitehead, and Joshua B Grubbs, "Culture Wars and COVID-19 Conduct: Christian Nationalism, Religiosity, and Americans' Behavior during the Coronavirus Pandemic," *Journal for the Scientific Study of Religion* 59, no. 3 (2020).

14. Perry, Whitehead, and Grubbs, "Culture Wars and COVID-19 Conduct."

15. In a recent study, Whitehead and Perry (2020) found that Christian nationalism was a powerful predictor of Americans being skeptical about vaccines and those who administer them. Andrew L Whitehead and Samuel L Perry, "How Culture Wars Delay Herd Immunity: Christian Nationalism and Anti-vaccine Attitudes," *Socius* 6 (2020). https://doi.org/10.1177/23780 23120977727, https://journals.sagepub.com/doi/abs/10.1177/23780 23120977727.

16. Samuel L Perry, Andrew L Whitehead, and Joshua B Grubbs, "Save the Economy, Liberty, and Yourself: Christian Nationalism and Americans' Views on Government COVID-19 Restrictions," *Sociology of Religion* (2020). https://doi.org/10.1093/socrel/sraa047, https://doi.org/10.1093/socrel/sraa047.

17. Chumley, *Socialists Don't Sleep: Christians Must Rise or America Will Fall*.
18. Dinesh D'Souza, *United States of Socialism: Who's Behind It. Why It's Evil. How to Stop It* (New York: All Points Books, 2020).
19. Lilliana Mason, *Uncivil Agreement: How Politics Became Our Identity* (Chicago: University of Chicago Press, 2018).

*Chapter 2*

1. Nikole Hannah-Jones, *The 1619 Project: A New Origin Story* (New York: One World, 2021); J Brian Charles, "The New York Times 1619 Project Is Reshaping the Conversation on Slavery. Conservatives Hate It," *Vox* (August 20, 2019). https://www.vox.com/identities/2019/8/19/20812238/1619-project-slavery-conservatives.
2. 1776 Commission, *1776 Report*, The White House (Washington, DC, 2021), https://trumpwhitehouse.archives.gov/briefings-statements/1776-commission-takes-historic-scholarly-step-restore-understanding-greatness-american-founding/; Gillian Brockell, "'A Hack Job,' 'Outright Lies': Trump Commission's '1776 Report' Outrages Historians," *Washington Post* (Washington, DC), January 20, 2021, https://www.washingtonpost.com/history/2021/01/19/1776-report-historians-trump/.
3. A comprehensive overview may be found in Ronald Takaki, *A Different Mirror: A History of Multicultural America*, 2nd. rev. ed. (Boston: Little, Brown and Company, 2008).Karen Brodkin, *How Jews Became White Folks and What That Says about Race in America* (New Brunswick, NJ: Rutgers University Press, 1998); Eric L Goldstein, *The Price of Whiteness: Jews, Race, and American Identity* (Princeton, NJ: Princeton University Press, 2019).
4. Gary B Nash, *Red, White, and Black: The Peoples of Early America* (Englewood Cliffs, NJ: Prentice-Hall, 1982); Richard A Bailey, *Race and Redemption in Puritan New England* (Oxford: Oxford University Press, 2011).
5. Benjamin Quarles, *The Negro in the American Revolution* (Chapel Hill: Omohundro Institute and University of North Carolina Press, 2012); Gary B Nash, *Race and Revolution* (Lanham, MD: Rowman & Littlefield, 1990); Sylvia R Frey, *Water from the Rock: Black Resistance in a Revolutionary Age* (Princeton, NJ: Princeton University Press, 2020).
6. The literature on Puritanism is massive. Helpful introductions include Michael P Winship, *Hot Protestants: A History of Puritanism in England and America* (New Haven, CT: Yale University Press, 2019); Francis J Bremer, *Puritanism: A Very Short Introduction* (Oxford: Oxford University Press, 2009); Jim Sleeper, "Our Puritan Heritage," *Democracy*, no. 37 (2015). https://democracyjournal.org/magazine/37/our-puritan-heritage/

7. Sacvan Bercovitch, *Typology and Early American Literature* (n.p.: University of Massachusetts Press, 1972); Thomas M Davis, "The Exegetical Traditions of Puritan Typology," *Early American Literature* 5, no. 1 (1970).Stephen Foster, *The Long Argument: English Puritanism and the Shaping of New England Culture, 1570–1700* (Chapel Hill: University of North Carolina Press, 1991); Francis J Bremer, *The Puritan Experiment: New England Society from Bradford to Edwards* (Lebanon, NH: University Press of New England, 1995); Nicholas Guyatt, *Providence and the Invention of the United States, 1607–1876* (New York: Cambridge University Press, 2007).

8. Robert Middlekauff, *The Mathers: Three Generations of Puritan Intellectuals, 1596–1728* (Berkeley: University of California Press, 1999); Jill Lepore, *The Name of War: King Philip's War and the Origins of American Identity,* 1st Vintage Books ed. (New York: Vintage Books, 1999).Cotton Mather, *Magnalia Christi Americana; or, The Ecclesiastical History of America* (Hartford, CT: W.S. Williams, 1855).William Bradford, *Bradford's History of Plymouth Planation, 1606–1646* (New York: Barnes and Noble, 1982); Susan Juster, *Sacred Violence in Early America* (Philadelphia: University of Pennsylvania Press, 2016); Alfred A Cave, *The Pequot War* (Amherst: University of Massachusetts Press, 1996).

9. On the history of apocalpytic thought within Protestantism: Irena Backus, *Reformation Readings of the Apocalypse: Geneva, Zurich, and Wittenberg* (Oxford: Oxford University Press, 2000); Paul Kenneth Christianson, *Reformers and Babylon: English Apocalyptic Visions from the Reformation to the Eve of the Civil War* (Toronto: University of Toronto Press, 1978); Fred Anderson and Andrew Cayton, *The Dominion of War: Empire and Liberty in North America, 1500–2000* (London: Penguin, 2005).

10. John Cotton, *God's Promise to His Plantations* (Boston: Reprinted by Samuel Green and are to be sold by John Usher, 1686); Kathryn N Gray, *John Eliot and the Praying Indians of Massachusetts Bay: Communities and Connections in Puritan New England* (Lewisburg, PA: Bucknell University Press, 2013); Richard Cogley, *John Eliot's Mission to the Indians before King Philip's War* (Cambridge, MA: Harvard University Press, 1999); Robert F Berkhofer, *The White Man's Indian: Images of the American Indian, from Columbus to the Present* (New York: Vintage, 1979). Lepore, *The Name of War: King Philip's War and the Origins of American Identity.*

11. On Williams's life, theology and politics, see Edmund Sears Morgan, *Roger Williams; the Church and the State,* 1st ed. (New York: Harcourt, 1967); James A Warren, *God, War, and Providence: The Epic Struggle of Roger Williams and the Narragansett Indians Against the Puritans of New England* (New York: Simon and Schuster, 2018); Teresa M Bejan, *Mere Civility* (Cambridge, MA: Harvard University Press, 2017).

12. Margaret Ellen Newell, *Brethren by Nature: New England Indians, Colonists, and the Origins of American Slavery* (Ithaca, NY: Cornell University Press, 2015). Nicholas P Canny, "The Ideology of English Colonization: From Ireland to America," *The William and Mary Quarterly* 30, no. 4 (1973), https://doi.org/ 10.2307/1918596, http://www.jstor.org/stable/1918596; Alden T Vaughan, *Roots of American Racism: Essays on the Colonial experience* (Oxford: Oxford University Press, 1995);.Rebecca Anne Goetz, *The Baptism of Early Virginia: How Christianity Created Race* (Baltimore: Johns Hopkins University Press, 2016); Philip Joseph Deloria, *Playing indian* (New Haven, CT: Yale University Press, 1998).

13. Stuart B Schwartz, *Tropical Babylons: Sugar and the Making of the Atlantic World, 1450–1680* (Chapel Hill: University of North Carolina Press, 2004). http://www.loc.gov/catdir/toc/ecip0413/2004001752.html.

14. Morgan Godwyn, *The Negro's & Indians Advocate* (London: Printed for the author, by J.D., 1680); David N Livingstone, *Adam's Ancestors. Race, Religion and the Politics of Human Origins* (Baltimore: Johns Hopkins University Press, 2008).

15. Whitford, *The Curse of Ham in the Early Modern Era: the Bible and the Justifications for Slavery.*

16. Peter Stamatov, *The Origins of Global Humanitarianism: Religion, Empires, and Advocacy* (Cambridge: Cambridge University Press, 2013). Samuel Sewall, *The Selling of Joseph a Memorial* (Boston of the Massachusetts: Printed by Bartholomew Green, and John Allen, 1700); William Lloyd Garrison, "Garrison's First Anti-Slavery Address in Boston," *Old South Leaflets*, no. 180 (1903).

17. On the complex political and cultural interchanges between native tribes and European colonists, see Kathleen DuVal, *The Native Ground* (Philadelphia: University of Pennsylvania Press, 2011); Richard White, *The Middle Ground: Indians, Empires, and Republics in the Great Lakes Region, 1650–1815* (Cambridge: Cambridge University Press, 2010).

18. Fred Anderson, *Crucible of War: The Seven Years' War and the Fate of Empire in British North America, 1754–1766* (New York: Knopf, 2000); Anderson and Cayton, *The Dominion of War: Empire and Liberty in North America, 1500–2000.*

19. Arthur H Buffinton, *The Second Hundred Years' War, 1689–1815* (New York: Holt, 1939).

20. Anderson, *Crucible of War: the Seven Years' War and the Fate of Empire in British North America, 1754–1766.*

21. Tyler Stovall, "White Freedom," in *White Freedom* (Princeton, NJ: Princeton University Press, 2021).

22. Linda Colley, *Britons: Forging the Nation, 1707–1837* (New Haven, CT: Yale University Press, 1992).

23. Thomas S Kidd, *The Protestant Interest: New England after Puritanism* (New Haven, CT: Yale University Press, 2004).

24. So-called captivity narratives—the first form of popular literature in the British colonies—described purported violations of white British Protestant bodies and consciences by "savages" and "Jesuits" in sometimes lurid detail. June Namias, *White Captives: Gender and eEhnicity on the American Frontier* (Chapel Hill: University of North Carolina Press, 1993); Pauline Turner Strong, *Captive Selves, Captivating Others: The Politics and Poetics of Colonial American Captivity Narratives* (New York: Routledge, 2018).

25. Nash, *Red, White, and Black: The Peoples of Early America.*

26. This ideal was propagated via popular culture. The hero of James Fenimore Cooper's "Leatherstocking Tales" (1827–1841)—America's first popular novels—was Natty Bumpo, an "Indian scout." In this myth, the rise of the scout was closely linked to the "vanishing" of the "Indian"—as if decimation and expropriation of native populations had nothing to do with the expansion of European colonialism. This part of the new American myth was first brought to the stage by the actor Edwin Forrest, who played the role of native chief, Metamora, in the one of the first popular plays in the United States, "The Last of the Wampanoags." As if to underline the savagery of the white American, Forrest projected a hyper-masculine image and stoked a widely publicized feud with the British Shakespearean actor, William MacReady, whom he castigated as weak and effeminate. As if to add an exclamation point to the affair, their rivalry eventually culminated in the mass fisticuff known as the Astor Place Riot. If the British version of white Christian nationalism was linked to a certain idea of white Protestant freedom, then the American version was also linked to a certain idea of white male violence. Deloria, *Playing Indian*; Lepore, *The Name of War: King Philip's War and the Origins of American Identity.*

27. This was how the political philosophers of Republican Rome had understood freedom, too. And Roman thought had a deep influence on Revolutionary ideology. Bailyn, *The Ideological Origins of the American Revolution*; Gordon S. Wood and Institute of Early American History and Culture (Williamsburg, VA), *The Creation of the American Republic, 1776–1787* (Chapel Hill: Published for the Institute of Early American History and Culture at Williamsburg, VA, 1969); Quentin Skinner, *Liberty before Liberalism* (Cambridge: Cambridge University Press, 1998).

28. Frey, *Water from the Rock: Black Resistance in a Revolutionary Age*; Quarles, *The Negro in the American Revolution.*

29. Gary B Nash, *Warner Mifflin: Unflinching Quaker Abolitionist* (Philadelphia: University of Pennsylvania Press, 2016); Donald J D'Elia, "Benjamin Rush: Philosopher of the American Revolution," *Transactions of the American Philosophical Society* 64, no. 5 (1974), http://www.jstor.org/stable/1006202.

30. for the following reasons: (1) The American Revolution greatly strengthened white antislavery sentiment, also in the South; (2) The two states whose economies depended most heavily on slavery—Georgia and South Carolina—were also the two states whose security dependent most heavily on union; (3) Slave owners could have been "compensated," and reparations given to the formerly enslaved, in the form of land in the trans-Appalachian West. Nash, *Race and Revolution*.

31. Heather Cox Richardson, *West from Appomattox: The Reconstruction of America after the Civil War* (New Haven, CT: Yale University Press, 2007); William D Carrigan and Clive Webb, *Forgotten Dead: Mob Violence against Mexicans in the United States, 1848–1928* (Oxford: Oxford University Press, 2013); Matthew McCullough, *The Cross of War: Christian Nationalism and US Expansion in the Spanish-American War* (Madison: University of Wisconsin Press, 2014); Beth Lew-Williams, *The Chinese Must Go: Violence, Exclusion, and the Making of the Alien in America* (Cambridge, MA: Harvard University Press, 2018).

32. Erika Lee, *America for Americans: A History of Xenophobia in the United States* (New York: Basic Books, 2019); Laura E Gómez, *Manifest Destinies: The Making of the Mexican American Race* (New York: NYU Press, 2018).

33. For a brief introduction to the Reconstruction era: Eric Foner, *A Short History of Reconstruction, 1863–1877*, 1st ed. (New York: Harper & Row, 1990); Heather Cox Richardson, *How the South Won the Civil War: Oligarchy, Democracy, and the Continuing Fight for the Soul of America* (New York: Oxford University Press, 2020); Charles Reagan Wilson, *Baptized in Blood: The Religion of the Lost Cause, 1865–1920* (Athens: University of Georgia Press, 1983); Ty Seidule, *Robert E. Lee and Me: A Southerner's Reckoning with the Myth of the Lost Cause* (New York: MacMillan, 2021); Karen L Cox, *Dixie's Daughters: The United Daughters of the Confederacy and the Preservation of Confederate Culture* (Gainesville: University of Florida Press, 2019).

34. Philip Gorski, "Trump's Rise and Fall Unified the Two Most Pernicious, Racist Myths About America," *NBCThink* (January 29, 2021). https://www.nbcn ews.com/think/opinion/trump-s-rise-fall-unified-two-most-pernicious-rac ist-myths-ncna1255880.

35. James H Moorhead, *World without End: Mainstream American Protestant Visions of the Last Things, 1880–1925*, vol. 28 (Bloomington: Indiana University Press, 1999); Thomas R Hietala, *Manifest Design: American Exceptionalism and Empire* (Ithaca, NY: Cornell University Press, 2003); Reginald Horsman, *Race and Manifest Destiny: The Origins of American Racial Anglo-Saxonism* (Cambridge, MA: Harvard University Press, 1981).

36. Karen E Fields and Barbara Jeanne Fields, *Racecraft: The Soul of Inequality in American Life* (London: Verso, 2014); Terence Keel, *Divine Variations* (Stanford, CA: Stanford University Press, 2020).

37. Horsman, *Race and Manifest Destiny: The Origins of American Racial Anglo-Saxonism*; Goldstein, *The Price of Whiteness: Jews, Race, and American Identity*; Matthew Frye Jacobson, *Whiteness of a Different Color: European Immigrants and the Alchemy of Race* (Cambridge, MA: Harvard University Press, 1998); David R Roediger, *The Wages of Whiteness: Race and the Making of the American Working Class*, The Haymarket series (London: Verso, 1991); Thomas A Guglielmo, *White on Arrival: Italians, Race, Color, and Power in Chicago, 1890–1945* (New York: Oxford University Press, 2003). Nancy Isenberg, *White Trash* (New York: Viking, 2016).

38. Gordon S Wood, *Empire of Liberty: A History of the Early Republic, 1789–1815* (Oxford: Oxford University Press, 2009).

39. Daniel Immerwahr, *How to Hide an Empire: A Short History of the Greater United States* (New York: Farrar, Straus and Giroux, 2019); Duncan Bell, *Dreamworlds of Race: Empire and the Utopian Destiny of Anglo-America* (Princeton, NJ: Princeton University Press, 2020).

40. Donald G Mathews, *At the Altar of Lynching: Burning Sam Hose in the American South* (Cambridge: Cambridge University Press, 2017); Walter White, *Rope and Faggot: A Biography of Judge Lynch* (Notre Dame, IN: University of Notre Dame Pess, 2002); James H Cone, *The Cross and the Lynching Tree* (Ossining, NY: Orbis Books, 2011).

41. Lew-Williams, *The Chinese Must Go: Violence, Exclusion, and the Making of the Alien in America*; Carrigan and Webb, *Forgotten Dead: Mob Biolence against Mexicans in the United States, 1848–1928*.

42. Kelly J Baker, *The Gospel According to the Klan: The KKK's Appeal to Protestant America, 1915–1930* (Lawrence: University Press of Kansas, 2011). Kevin M Kruse, *White Flight: Atlanta and the Making of Modern Conservatism*, vol. 89 (Princeton, NJ: Princeton University Press, 2013).

43. Neil Foley, *The White Scourge: Mexicans, Blacks, and Poor Whites in Texas Cotton Culture*, vol. 2 (Berkeley and Los Angeles: University of California Press, 1998); Heather D Curtis, *Holy Humanitarians: American Evangelicals and Global Aid* (Cambridge, MA: Harvard University Press, 2018); Bell, *Dreamworlds of Race: Empire and the Utopian Destiny of Anglo-America*; Markku Ruotsila, *The Origins of Christian Anti-internationalism: Conservative Evangelicals and the League of Nations* (Washington, DC: Georgetown University Press, 2007).

44. Angie Maxwell and Todd Shields, *The Long Southern Strategy: How Chasing White Voters in the South Changed American Politics* (Oxford: Oxford University Press, 2019); Daniel K Williams, *Defenders of the Unborn: The Pro-Life Movement before Roe v. Wade* (New York: Oxford University Press, 2015).

45. Matthew Avery Sutton, *American Apocalypse* (Cambridge, MA: Harvard University Press, 2014); Boyer, *When Time Shall Be No More: Prophecy Belief in Modern American Culture*.

46. Joseph E Lowndes, *From the New Deal to the New Right: Race and the Southern Origins of Modern Conservatism* (New Haven, CT: Yale University Press, 2008); Joseph Crespino, *Strom Thurmond's America* (New York: Macmillan, 2012); Dan T Carter, *From George Wallace to Newt Gingrich: Race in the Conservative Counterrevolution, 1963–1994* (Baton Rouge: Louisiana State University Press, 1996).

47. Michael O Emerson and Christian Smith, *Divided by Faith: Evangelical Religion and the Problem of Race in America* (New York: Oxford University Press, 2001).

48. Sara Moslener, *Virgin Nation: Sexual Purity and American Adolescence* (New York: Oxford University Press, 2015); Sophie Bjork-James, *The Divine Institution: White Evangelicalism's Politics of the Family* (New Brunswick, NJ: Rutgers University Press, 2021); R Marie Griffith, *Moral Combat: How Sex Divided American Christians and Fractured American Politics* (New York: Basic Books, 2017).

49. Kruse, *One Nation under God: How Corporate America /invented Christian America.*

50. Crespino, *Strom Thurmond's America.*

51. Kruse, *White Flight: Atlanta and the Making of Modern Conservatism,* 89.

52. Susan Friend Harding, *The Book of Jerry Falwell: Fundamentalist Language and Politics* (Princeton, NJ: Princeton University Press, 2000).

53. Michael J McVicar, *Christian Reconstruction: RJ Rushdoony and American Religious Conservatism* (Chapel Hill: University of North Carolina Press, 2015); Julie Ingersoll, *Building God's Kingdom: Inside the World of Christian Reconstruction* (New York: Oxford University Press, 2015).

54. Gary North, *Christian Economics in One Lesson,* 2nd ed. (Dallas, TX: Point Five Press, 2020).

55. James D Bratt, "Abraham Kuyper, J Gresham Machen, and the Dynamics of Reformed Anti-Modernism," *Journal of Presbyterian History* 75, no. 4 (1997).

56. Tim Alberta, "The Financial Whisperer to Trump's America," *Politico Magazine* (March/April 2018). https://www.politico.com/magazine/story/2018/03/11/radio-dave-ramsey-2018-trump-217229; Bob Smietana, "Is Dave Ramsey's Empire the 'Best Place to Work in America'? Say No and You're Out," *Religion News Service* (January 15, 2021). https://religionnews.com/2021/01/15/dave-ramsey-is-tired-of-being-called-a-jerk-for-his-stands-on-sex-and-covid/; Susan Drury, "The Gospel According to Dave," *Nashville Scene,* May 31, 2007, https://www.nashvillescene.com/news/article/13014787/the-gospel-accord ing-to-dave; Matthew Paul Turner, "Spies, Cash, and Fear: Inside Christian Money Guru Dave Ramsey's Media Witch Hunt," *The Daily Beast* (September 11, 2018). https://www.thedailybeast.com/spies-cash-and-fear-inside-christ ian-money-guru-dave-ramseys-social-media-witch-hunt; Helaine Olen, "The Prophet," *Pacific Standard Magazine* (June 14, 2017). https://psmag.com/soc ial-justice/prophet-dave-ramsey-personal-finance-67269.

57. Smietana, "Is Dave Ramsey's Empire the 'Best Place to Work in America'? Say No and You're Out."

58. Greg Grandin, *The End of the Myth: From the Frontier to the Border Wall in the Mind of America* (New York: Metropolitan Books, 2019).

Chapter 3

1. Jacob S Hacker and Paul Pierson, *Let Them Eat Tweets: How the Right Rules in an Age of Extreme Inequality* (New York: Liveright Publishing, 2020).

2. Kristin Kobes Du Mez, *Jesus and John Wayne: How White Evangelicals Corrupted a Faith and Fractured a Nation* (New York: Liveright Publishing, 2020); Kathryn Joyce, *Quiverfull: Inside the Christian Patriarchy Movement* (Boston: Beacon Press, 2009).

3. Gerardo Martí, *American Blindspot: Race, Class, Religion, and the Trump Presidency.*

4. Kim Phillips-Fein, *Invisible Hands: The Businessmen's Crusade against the New Deal* (New York: WW Norton & Company, 2010); Lowndes, *From the New Deal to the New Right: Race and the Southern Origins of Modern Conservatism*; Kruse, *One Nation under God: How Corporate America Invented Christian America*; Butler, *White Evangelical Racism: The Politics of Morality in America.*

5. Jill Lepore, *The Whites of Their Eyes: The Tea Party's Revolution and the Battle over American History* (Princeton, NJ: Princeton University Press, 2011), p. 4.

6. Steve Gooch, "Tea Party: Wednesday, April 15, 2009—Photo Gallery," *The Oklahoman* (Tulsa), April 15, 2009. https://www.oklahoman.com/gallery/500846/tea-party-wednesday-april-15-2009%5d.

7. "2009," accessed April 1, 2021, https://www.everypixel.com/image-7323 367015791036067 (FORT MYERS, FL.—APRIL 15: Tax Day Tea Party event participants show their signs in Ft. Myers on April 15, 2009 in Fort Myers.).

8. Theda Skocpol and Vanessa Williamson, *The Tea Party and the Remaking of Republican Conservatism* (New York: Oxford University Press, 2012); David Brody, *The Teavangelicals: The Inside Story of How the Evangelicals and the Tea Party Are Taking Back America* (Grand Rapids, MI: Zondervan, 2012); Lepore, *The Whites of Their Eyes*; Ruth Braunstein, *Prophets and Patriots: Faith in Democracy across the Political Divide* (Berkeley and Los Angeles: University of California Press, 2017).

9. Ruth Braunstein and Malaena Taylor, "Is the Tea Party a "Religious" Movement? Religiosity in the Tea Party versus the Religious Right," *Sociology of Religion* 78, no. 1 (2017).

10. Angelia R Wilson and Cynthia Burack, "'Where Liberty Reigns and God Is Supreme': The Christian Right and the Tea Party Movement," *New Political*

*Science* 34, no. 2 (2012); Melissa Deckman et al., "Faith and the Free Market: Evangelicals, the Tea Party, and Economic Attitudes," *Politics & Religion* 10, no. 1 (2017).

11. Eric D Knowles et al., "Race, Ideology, and the Tea Party: A Longitudinal Study," *PLoS One* 8, no. 6 (2013).

12. Devin Burghart and Leonard Zeskind, *Tea Party Nationalism: A Critical Examination of the Tea Party Movement and the Size, Scope, and Focus of Its National Factions*, (Kansas City, MO: Institute for Research & Education on Human Rights 2010). https://www.irehr.org/2010/10/12/tea-party-nati onalism-report-pdf/.

13. David Nakamura, "Trump Recycles Discredited Islamic Pigs' Blood Tale after Terrorist Attack in Barcelona," *Washington Post* (Washington, D.C.), August 17, 2017, https://www.washingtonpost.com/news/post-politics/wp/2017/ 08/17/trump-recycles-discredited-islamic-pigs-blood-tale-after-terrorist-att ack-in-barcelona.

14. Nurith Aizenman, "Trump Wishes We Had More Immigrants from Norway. Turns Out We Once Did," *NPR* (January 12, 2018). https://www.npr.org/ sections/goatsandsoda/2018/01/12/577673191/trump-wishes-we-had-more-immigrants-from-norway-turns-out-we-once-did.

15. Jane Tompkins, *West of Everything: The Inner Life of Westerns* (Oxford: Oxford University Press, 1993).

16. Du Mez, *Jesus and John Wayne*.

17. Clifford Putney, *Muscular Christianity: Manhood and Sports in Protestant America, 1880–1920* (Cambridge, MA: Harvard University Press, 2009).

18. In the words of Owen Strachan and Mark Driscoll, respectively. See Molly Worthen, "Who Would Jesus Smack Down," *New York Times Magazine* (January 6, 2009). https://www.nytimes.com/2009/01/11/magazine/ 11punk-t.html and https://twitter.com/ostrachan/status/122977312204 9658882. On race and superheroes, see Edward J Blum and Paul Harvey, *The Color of Christ: The Son of God and the Saga of Race in America* (Chapel Hill: UNC Press Books, 2012). Jewett and Lawrence, *Captain America and the Crusade against Evil: The Dilemma of Zealous Nationalism* (Grand Rapids, MI: Eerdmans, 2004).

19. Andrew R Lewis, *The Rights Turn in Conservative Christian Politics: How Abortion Transformed the Culture Wars* (New York: Cambridge University Press, 2017).

20. Peter Wade, "In a Desperate Rant, Trump Nonsensically Says Biden Will 'Hurt God, Hurt the Bible,'" *Rolling Stone* (August 6, 2020). https://www.rollingst one.com/politics/politics-news/trump-says-biden-will-hurt-god-hurt-the-bible-1040799/.

21. Samuel L Perry, Landon Schnabel, and Joshua B Grubbs, "Christian Nationalism, Perceived Anti-Christian Discrimination, and Prioritizing

'Religious Freedom' in the 2020 Presidential Election," *Nations and Nationalism* (2021), https://doi.org/10.1111.

22. Fabiola Cineas, "Donald Trump Is the Accelerant", *Vox* (January 9. 2021). https://www.vox.com/21506029/trump-violence-tweets-racist-hate-speech.

23. Matt Walsh, *Church of Cowards: A Wake-Up Call to Complacent Christians* (New York: Simon and Schuster, 2020).

24. Aaron Griffith, *God's Law and Order* (Cambridge, MA: Harvard University Press, 2020).

25. Butler, *White Evangelical Racism.*

26. Andrew Kaczynski, "Mike Huckabee Says He Doesn't Want "Stupid" People To Vote," *Buzzfeed News* (September 22, 2015). https://www.buzzfeednews. com/article/andrewkaczynski/mike-huckabee-says-less-stupid-people-sho uld-vot.

27. Glenn Elmers, "'Conservatism' Is No Longer Enough," *American Mind* (March 24 2021). https://americanmind.org/salvo/why-the-claremont-institute-is-not-conservative-and-you-shouldnt-be-either/.

28. Jack Kerwick, "Good People Must Be Dangerous People," *American Greatness* (April 12, 2021). https://amgreatness.com/2021/04/12/good-people-must-be-dangerous-people/.

*Chapter 4*

1. Corey Robin, *The Reactionary Mind: Conservatism from Edmund Burke to Sarah Palin* (Oxford: Oxford University Press, 2011).

2. Lee, *America for Americans: A history of Xenophobia in the United States.*

3. Jean Guerrero, "Trump's Re-election Strategy Is Torn from White Supremacist Playbooks," *The Guardian* (Manchester) (September 9 2020). https://www. theguardian.com/commentisfree/2020/sep/09/trumps-reelection-strat egy-is-torn-from-white-supremacist-playbooks. Ann Coulter, *Adios, America: The Left's Plan to Turn Our Country into a Third World Hellhole* (New York: Simon and Schuster, 2015). Jonathan Chait, "Tucker Carlson Endorses White Supremacist Theory by Name," *New York Magazine* (April 9 2021). https:// nymag.com/intelligencer/2021/04/tucker-carlson-great-replacement-white-supremacist-immigration-fox-news-racism.html.

4. Musa al-Gharbi, "White Men Swung to Biden. Trump Made Gains with Black and Latino voters. Why?," *The Guardian* (Manchester) (November 14 2020). https://www.theguardian.com/commentisfree/2020/nov/14/joe-biden-trump-black-latino-republicans.

5. PRRI Staff, "Understanding QAnon's Connection to American Politics, Religion, and Media Consumption," *PRRI* (May 26 2021). https://www.prri. org/research/qanon-conspiracy-american-politics-report/.

6. Baker, *The Gospel According to the Klan: The KKK's Appeal to Protestant America, 1915–1930*.

7. Jonathan P Herzog, *The Spiritual-Industrial Complex: America's Religious Battle against Communism in the Early Cold War* (Oxford: Oxford University Press, 2011); Steven P Miller, *Billy Graham and the Rise of the Republican South* (Philadelphia: University of Pennsylvania Press, 2011).

8. Robert P Saldin and Steven M Teles, *Never Trump: The Revolt of the Conservative Elites* (New York: Oxford University Press, 2020).

9. Quint Forgey, "Trump: 'I'm a nationalist,'" *Politico* (October 22, 2018). https://www.politico.com/story/2018/10/22/trump-nationalist-926745. https://know-your-enemy-1682b684.simplecast.com/episodes/teaser-the-1776-project This wasn't just rhetoric to rally the crowd. In fact, Trump told world representatives as much in his 2019 United Nations address, declaring "The future does not belong to globalists."

10. Sarah Pulliam Bailey, "'God Is Not Against Building Walls!' The Sermon Trump Heard from Robert Jeffress before his Inauguration," *The Washington Post*, January 20, 2017, https://www.washingtonpost.com/news/acts-of-faith/wp/2017/01/20/god-is-not-against-building-walls-the-sermon-don ald-trump-heard-before-his-inauguration/;Brandon Showalter, "Wayne Grudem: Trump's Border Wall 'Morally Good' Because Bible Cities Had Walls," *The Christian Post*, July 2 2018, https://www.christianpost.com/news/wayne-grudem-trump-border-wall-morally-good-bible-cities.html. Paul Harvey, "The Bounds of Their Habitation: Race and Religion in American History," *Journal of American Studies* 51, no. 1 (2017).

11. Christian nationalism is the key. We've already seen how Christian nationalist ideology corresponded to trusting Donald Trump above all scientific and medical experts during the COVID-19 pandemic (Chapter 1). And affirming Christian nationalism was the most powerful predictor that white Americans absolved Trump of all blame for the Capitol insurrection (Chapter 3).

12. Tom McCarthy, "'I Am the Chosen One': With Boasts and insults, Trump Sets New Benchmark for incoherence," *The Guardian* (Manchester) (August 21 2019). https://www.theguardian.com/us-news/2019/aug/21/trump-press-conference-greenland-jewish-democrats.

13. Tola Mbakwe, "Donald Trump: 'I Am the Chosen one,'" *Premier Christian News* (London) (August 22 2019). https://premierchristian.news/en/news/article/donald-trump-i-am-the-chosen-one.

14. John General and Richa Naik, "QAnon Is Spreading amongst Evangelicals. These Pastors Are Trying to Stop It," *CNN Business*, May 23 2021, https://www.cnn.com/2021/05/23/business/qanon-evangelical-pastors/index.html.

15. Robert A Dahl, *On Democracy* (New Haven, CT: Yale University Press, 2020); Benjamin Isakhan, "The Complex and Contested History of Democracy," in

*The Edinburgh Companion to the History of Democracy*, ed. Stephen Stockwell and Benjamin Isakhan (Edinburgh: Edinburgh University Press, 2012).

16. Steven Elliott Grosby, *Nationalism: A Very Short Introduction*, p. 134 (Oxford: Oxford University Press, 2005).

17. Zachary B Wolf, "The 5 Key Elements of Trump's Big Lie and Hit Came to Be," *CNN Politics*, May 19 2021. https://www.cnn.com/2021/05/19/politics/donald-trump-big-lie-explainer/index.html.

18. Alexander Keyssar, *The Right to Vote: The Contested History of Democracy in the United States* (New York: Basic Books, 2009); Allan J Lichtman, *The Embattled Vote in America* (Cambridge, MA: Harvard University Press, 2018).

19. Sam Levine, "'It Can't Be That Easy': US Conservative Group Brags about Role in Making Voting Harder," *The Guardian* (May 13 2021).

20. Isabella Zou, "Texas Senate Bill Seeks to Strip Required Lessons on People of Color and Women from 'Critical Race Theory' Law," *Texas Tribune* ( July 9 2021).

21. Sohrab Ahmari, "Against David French-ism," *First Things* (May 29 2019). https://www.firstthings.com/web-exclusives/2019/05/against-david-french-ism.

22. Jason Blakely, "The Integralism of Adrian Vermeule," *Commonweal* (October 5 2020). https://www.commonwealmagazine.org/not-catholic-enough; James Chappel, "Nudging Toward Theocracy: Adrian Vermeule's War on Liberalism," *Dissent* (2020).

23. Rich Lowry, *The Case for Nationalism: How It Made Us Powerful, United and Free* (New York: Broadside Books, 2019).

24. Peter J Leithart, *Defending Constantine: The Twilight of an Empire and the Dawn of Christendom* (Downers Grove, IL: InterVarsity Press, 2010).

25. Julie L. Ingersoll, *Building God's Kingdom: Inside the World of Christian Reconstruction* (New York: Oxford University Press, 2015) ; Michael J. McVicar, *Christian Reconstruction: RJ Rushdoony and American Religious Conservatism* (Chapel Hill, NC: University of North Carolina Press, 2015); Sara Diamond, *Roads to Dominion: Right-Wing Movements and Political Power in the United States* (New York: Guilford Press, 1995).

26. Michael Anton and Curtis Yarvin, "The Stakes: The American Monarchy?," *The American Mind* ( June 18 2021).

27. Cristóbal Rovira Kaltwasser et al., *The Oxford Handbook of Populism* (Oxford: Oxford University Press, 2017); Mark Juergensmeyer, "Religious Nationalism in a Global World," *Religions* 10, no. 2 (2019).

28. Nadia Marzouki, Duncan McDonnell, and Olivier Roy, *Saving the People: How Populists Hijack Religion* (Oxford: Oxford University Press, 2016).

29. Steven Levitsky and Daniel Ziblatt, *How Democracies Die* (New York: Crown, 2018).

30. Political scientists Andrew Gelman and Pierre-Antoine Kremp estimate that, because the electoral college disproportionately advantages rural red states, per voter, it ultimately gives whites 16% more voting power than Blacks and 28% more power than Latinos. Andrew Gelman and Pierre-Antoine Kremp, "The Electoral College Magnifies the Power of White Voters," *Vox, December* 16 (2016).

31. Ruth Ben-Ghiat, "Strongmen: How They Rise, Why They Succeed, How They Fall" (London: Taylor & Francis, 2021).

32. Pierre L Van den Berghe, "South Africa after Thirty Years," *Social Dynamics* 16, no. 2 (1990).

33. David A French, *Divided We Fall: America's Secession Threat and How to Restore Our Nation* (New York: St. Martin's Press, 2020). On what that might look like, see the futuristic novel, Omar El Akkad, *American War* (New York: Vintage, 2017).

34. Thomas R Hietala, *Manifest Design: Anxious Aggrandizement in Late Jacksonian America* (Ithaca, NY: Cornell University Press, 1985); Edward J Blum, *Reforging the White Republic: Race, Religion, and American Nationalism, 1865–1898*, Conflicting Worlds (Baton Rouge: Louisiana State University Press, 2005). http://www.loc.gov/catdir/toc/ecip0422/2004021168.html; Elizabeth Hinton, *From the War on Poverty to the War on Crime: The Making of Mass Incarceration in America* (Cambridge, MA: Harvard University Press, 2016).

35. David A Hollinger, *After Cloven Tongues of Fire: Protestant Liberalism in Modern American History* (Princeton, NHJ: Princeton University Press, 2013).

36. Reinhart Koselleck, *Futures Past: On the Semantics of Historical Time* (New York: Columbia University Press, 2004).

37. Daniel Markovits, *The Meritocracy Trap: How America's Foundational Myth Feeds Inequality, Dismantles the Middle Class, and Devours the Elite* (New York: Penguin, 2019). Derek Thompson, "Workism Is Making Americans Miserable," *The Atlantic* (February 24, 2019). https://www.theatlantic.com/ideas/arch ive/2019/02/religion-workism-making-americans-miserable/583441/.

# INDEX

# INDEX